Physical Characteristics of th Affenpinscher

(from the American Kennel Club breed sta

Back: Short and level.

Tail: May be docked or natural. WITHDRAWN

Hindquarters: Rear angulation is moderate to match the front. From the side, hindlegs are set under the body to maintain a square appearance. Hocks—moderately angulated.

Coat: Dense hair, rough, harsh, and about 1 inch in length on the shoulders and body. The longer hair on the head, eyebrows and beard stands off and frames the face to emphasize the monkey-like expression.

Height: At the withers is 9.5 inches to 11.5 inches.

Color: Black, gray, silver, red, black and tan or belge are all acceptable.

Affenpinscher

By Jerome Cushman

Contents

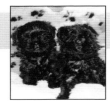

Training Your Affenpinscher 88

Begin with the basics of training the puppy and adult dog. Learn the principles of house-training the Affenpinscher, including the use of crates and basic scent instincts. Get started by introducing the pup to his collar and leash and progress to the basic commands. Find out about obedience classes and other activities.

Healthcare of Your Affenpinscher 115

By Lowell Ackerman DVM, DACVD
Become your dog's healthcare advocate and a well-educated canine keeper. Select a skilled and able veterinarian. Discuss pet insurance, vaccinations and infectious diseases, the neuter/spay decision and a sensible, effective plan for parasite control, including fleas, ticks and worms.

Showing Your Affenpinscher 144

Step into the center ring and find out about the world of showing pure-bred dogs. Here are the basics of AKC conformation, including how shows are organized and what's required for your dog to become a champion. Also presented are things to think about if you want to try showing and how to get started.

Photography by:

Alverson Photographers, Animal World Studio, Ashbey Photography, Janet Ashbey, Nancy Baybutt, Mary Bloom, Kim Booth, Paulette Braun, Alan and Sandy Carey, Carolina Biological Supply, Wendy Clark, David Dalton, Isabelle Français, Gay Glazbrook, Michael Graat, Earl Graham Studios, Bruce and Jeane Harkins, Holloway Photography, JC Photography, Carol Ann Johnson, Bill Jonas, Klein Photography, Kohler Photographers, Dr. Dennis Kunkel, Elizabeth Muir-Chamberlain, Debrah H. Muska (Animal Images), Tam C. Nguyen, Phototake, Jean Claude Revy, Nancy Spelke (Custom Dog Designs), R. Strempski, Charles Tatham and Alice van Kempen.

Illustrations by Patricia Peters.

The author is indebted to the following individuals for their contribution to the text of this book: Jo Ann White, Bardi McLennan and Nona Kilgore Bauer.

KENNEL CLUB BOOKS® AFFENPINSCHER
ISBN: 1-59378-335-3

Copyright © 2006 • Kennel Club Books LLC
308 Main Street, Allenhurst, NJ 07711 USA
Cover Design Patented: US 6,435,559 B2 • Printed in South Korea

Here is "Cosmos," the top-winning Affenpinscher in the history of the breed. Formally he's Ch. Yarrow's Super Nova, bred by Beth Sweigart and Letisha Wubbel and owned by Dr. and Mrs. William Truesdale.

HISTORY OF THE

AFFENPINSCHER

EARLY HISTORY OF THE BREED
The Affenpinscher has its origin in
Germany. The progenitor of the
breed was probably a rough-coated
little ratter that survived in the
central European countries by its
clever personality and its rodent-
killing abilities. The Flemish artist
Jan Van Eyck (1390–1441) included
in his painting *The Marriage of
Giovanni Arnolfini and Giovanna
Cenami* a scruffy terrier-type dog,
placed facing the audience between
the newlyweds. This is an example
of the type of dog that probably was
the ancestor of both the Brussels
Griffon and the Affenpinscher.
Albrecht Durer (1471–1525) from
Nuremberg, Germany included a
small dog in several of his woodcuts
that suggest the existence of this
"Long-haired Dwarf Terrier." Seven-
teenth-century painter Gabriel
Metsu (1629–1667) portrayed a little
dog that looks very much like our
contemporary Affenpinscher in his
celebrated work *A Soldier Receiving
a Young Woman,* which today hangs
in the Louvre. Other dog enthusiasts
claim these representations as early
examples of their own breeds. One
thing certain is that a small rough-

coated household dog similar to the
Affenpinscher existed and was
admired for several centuries.

In addition to the Affenpinscher,
the Miniature Pinscher, the Miniature Schnauzer and the Brussels
Griffon were all probably generated
from this same type of dog. Later,
with the infusion of other breeds
plus selective breeding, the specifics
of breed type developed and were
promoted. For example, breeders
crossed in the Pug to develop the
Brussels Griffon, while others
added the English Black and Tan
Terrier to create the Miniature
Pinscher. By adding a small, dark
schnauzer-type hunting dog from
southern Russia, the Miniature
Schnauzer was created. In each of
these breeds' histories there were
times when it became necessary to
cross back into the associated breeds
to keep the newer breed viable. In
any case, the Affenpinscher is an
old breed.

Official records or formal breeding programs for this breed did not
exist until the late 1800s. Dog show
records from the 1870s and '80s in
southern Germany, around Frankfurt
and Munich, reflect that the breed

> ### AFFENS IN ART
> One of the earliest visual records of the Affenpinscher's existence is in a woodcut by Albrecht Durer (1471–1525). A portrait of a French-owned Affenpinscher by the Dutch artist Charles Verlai sometime before 1890 indicates that by then the breed was already becoming known outside its native Germany. The Affenpinscher also appears in some paintings by the French artist Pierre Auguste Renoir (1841–1919).

was firmly established and exhibited. In an 1889 publication, *The Canine Chronicle,* there is a description of a special show in Frankfurt sponsored by a club for the German Toy Rat-terriers (Affenpinschers). "Affenpinscher" was first used for the name of the breed at this time. Until then the word "Affenpinscher" was used as an adjective. At this show there were classes for dogs weighing under 5 pounds and over 5 pounds. By the early 1900s these two size classifications seemed to disappear. The smaller

A Victorian-era postcard showing an Affenpinscher of early type. Courtesy of the author.

ones assumed the former nickname, Affenpinscher, with the larger type being absorbed into the Miniature Schnauzer breed. Instead of its earlier function of being a "ratter," the smaller Affenpinscher is more of a "mouser." However, even today a large specimen of between 13 to 16 inches might appear in a closely line-bred litter. These larger throwbacks generally have great personalities and are of good breed type, except for the size and the fact that their muzzles may be a bit longer. This larger type usually makes an excellent companion for a family with young children.

From Volume II (1903–1907) of the registration book for the German Pinscher-Schnauzer Club (PSK), the Affenpinscher is listed for the first time as a separate breed. Fourteen specimens are recorded. Except for during World War I (1914–1918), the numbers continued to thrive until 1939, with the majority of the breed coming from the area around Munich. It seems that the Affenpinscher reached a high point in the late '20s and early '30s. The people with wealth and fame in German society promoted the breed. It was often seen in dog acts on stage and in circuses. With the onset of World War II in 1939, the decline began, and the breed's popularity was never again the same in Germany. Of late, the number of Affenpinschers born annually in Germany remains only in the teens.

In early years the breed came in a variety of colors. Then under the leadership of the prominent breeder von Otto, a decision was made that a black coat best suited the personality of the breed. From 1917 to 1923, 60% of the Affenpinschers were of colors other than black. Gradually black became the predominant color. In 1935, 78% of the registered dogs were black. As late as 1954, 5% were still colors other than black. Now, throughout Europe and England, black is the preferred color, and no other color is encouraged or allowed to be exhibited. In North America the colors that were first described for the breed are accepted equally, and many of them are shown. However, the majority of Affens in America are black.

The dogs represented in photographs from the early 1900s closely resemble today's Affenpinschers. Obviously, the type for the breed was set early on and has been maintained over the years by a few devoted breeders around the world. It seems odd that this breed has never reached the popularity it deserves. Its greatest strides have been made in America and recently in England.

ENTER THE BRUSSELS GRIFFON

The Affenpinscher served as foundation stock for another toy breed, the Brussels Griffon, which descended from crosses between the Belgian street dog (Griffon D'Ecurie) and the Affenpinscher, with later crosses to the Pug and the Ruby Spaniel. During World War II, when Affenpinschers became almost extinct, German breeders crossed Affenpinschers back to the Brussels Griffon, resulting in undershot jaws and shorter muzzles. The modern Brussels Griffon is generally more outgoing than the Affenpinscher, with a shorter nose and rounder head. While black Brussels Griffons are permitted, that breed is usually red, belge or black and tan.

THE AFFENPINSCHER IN AMERICA

Affenpinschers were first listed in the American Kennel Club stud book in November 1936. At this time an abbreviated translation of the German standard was accepted as the American breed standard. The first entry in the stud book was for Nolli v Anwander. This was a German female imported in whelp by Mrs. Bessie Mally of Cicero, Illinois. The first male that she imported was Osko von der Franziskusklause. From 1936 to 1940, Mrs. Mally had 22 Affenpinschers listed in the stud books. During these years, 27 dogs were registered with the AKC. A few other enthusiasts also had imports or bred with Mrs. Mally's dogs. During this period Thelma D. Wolfe exhibited her dog, named Duke of Wolfe II. By some accounts this dog became a champion. However, October 1940 was the last Affenpinscher entry in the Stud Book for the next nine years. Sadly, there are no records or reasons given for this abrupt end of the breeding of Affenpinschers in America. Likely US involvement with the Allies in World War II and the accompanying hostilities toward all things German led to the Affenpinscher's decline in popularity. No one seems to know what happened to these early dogs, and none is found in the pedigrees of the later dogs in America.

The renowned dog fancier Mrs. Henrietta Proctor Donnell Reilly, of Larchmount, NY, continued the exhibiting of the breed during these years. Her German import Ger. Ch. Niki v. Zwergteufel won Best of Breed at the Westminster Dog Show for six consecutive years, from 1938–1943. Then a kennel mate of Niki, Ger. Ch. Everl v. d. Franziskusklause, won for the next four years through 1947. No record of Mrs. Reilly's kennel name, Etty Haven, is found in the stud books, so no breeding of her Affenpinschers was done or none of these offspring was registered.

The next American encounter with this breed was in 1949, when an import owned by Mrs. Evelyne Brody, Ch. Bub v. Anwander, became the first Affenpinscher champion according to American Kennel Club records. This dog also went on to become the first Affenpinscher to place in the Toy Group. During the next several years Mrs. Brody's kennel name, Cedarlawn, from Nashotah, Wisconsin, dominated the listings in the stud book. Many of the Affenpinschers today can trace their bloodlines back to the Cedarlawn dogs.

Soon Mrs. Walter Kauffmann and her daughters, Helga and Louisa, from Westwood, New Jersey, also imported dogs. Interestingly these later imports came from the same kennels in Germany from which Mrs. Mally had gotten her original dogs. The Kauffmanns, under the Walhof name, became prominent breeders and exhibitors. Helga Kauffmann exhibited extensively and had the top group-placing Affenpinschers for many years. Their champion Walhof Margaretenklause Ivy, a female, was the first Affenpinscher to win the Toy Group, and their Ch. Je-Bil's Yogi Bear was the first male Toy Group winner. Some of these early dogs produced colors other than black. When looking back at the AKC stud books, it seems that two of the Kauffmann imports, when bred together, produced reds. Ch. Kraus v. d. Margaretenklause and Ch. Blanka v. d. Charlottenhohe were the parents of Walhof Little Red Riding Hood. Later the Kauffmanns' Ch. Walhof Ivin was the first red champion, and

his littermate Ch. Walhof Boutonniere became the first black-and-tan champion. These two dogs were out of Ch. Walhof Margaretenklause Lee and Walhof Margaretenklause Jan.

MEET THE MONKEY TERRIER

In German, the word *affenmartig* means "monkey-like," and the word *pinscher* means "terrier." The Affenpinscher is sometimes called the "monkey terrier," and this may be how it got its alternative name. However, the "monkey" label may have come into common use simply because of the breed's bewhiskered and mischievous expression and amusing behavior. In France, the breed is often called the "Diablotin Moustachu," or the "mustached little devil," another clue to its behavior.

From Florence Strohmaier's successful Flo-Star kennels, here is seven-month-old Flo-Star's Little Tiam, who became one of Florence's important sires.

When Boutonniere was bred to Little Red Riding Hood they produced top-winning Ch. Walhof Ivy, a black-and-tan group winner, and Ch. Walhof Blackberry Brandi. With the help of Jerry Zalon they produced many dogs of colors other than black. From these early dogs the color genes can be traced into England and continental Europe today. The Kauffmanns were probably the most instrumental breeders in the development of the Affenpinscher in America. The Walhof prefix is behind nearly all of the dogs in North America and England.

Another important kennel that greatly influenced the breed in the '50s and '60s was Arthur and Mary Harrington's Aff-Airn kennels from Albany, New York. Aff-Airn continued on with what Mrs. Brody had begun. They also bred with the Walhof kennels. One among many notable dogs of their breeding, Ch. Aff-Airn Tag Along, made a significant contribution to the breed.

In 1958, Mrs. Florence Strohmaier became a friend of the Harringtons and started working with the Aff-Airn Affens. After the death of Mary and Arthur, Mrs. Strohmaier continued their lines but went out on her own under the name Flo-Star kennels. Her dogs continue to have an impact on the breed in the US, Canada, England, Ireland, Scotland, Holland and Germany. Ch. Flo-Star's Adam of Joy, a grandson of Ch. Walhof Boutonniere, is behind many of the top-winning and top-producing Affenpinschers. Am., Can. and Bermuda Ch. Flo-Star's Holy Terror and Am., Can., Bermuda and Dutch Ch. Flo-Star's Tandy Tane were some of Mrs. Strohmaier's important contributors to the breed. Ch. Flo-Star's Titus Tiberius, CD was one of the first conformation- and obedience-titled Affenpinschers to get Toy Group placements. Primarily known for her black dogs, Mrs. Strohmaier won Winners Dog and Winners Bitch at the 1997 national specialty with her red or wild boar Affens. The Flo-Star Affens are known for their typey heads and good substance. Until her death in 2005, Flo Strohmaier consistently remained involved with the Affenpinscher. Her 48 years in the breed stand as a legacy, making her involvement longer than that of any other breeder in America.

In the early 1960s, Tobin Jackson and D. V. Gibbs got their start in the breed from the Walhof and Aff-Airn kennels. Soon the Deer Run Affenpinschers from Frenchtown, New Jersey were making a mark in the dog world. Most American Affenpinschers have Deer Run bloodlines behind them. Jackson and Gibbs also wrote about the breed in *How to Raise and Train an Affenpinscher,* published in 1969, now out of print. Mr. Jackson also wrote interesting and informative articles for the magazine *Popular Dogs.* In the mid-'60s, Bonnie (Hawkins) Sellner began working with and showing the Deer Run dogs. Ms. Sellner has worked with several other kennels, helping with their breeding programs and exhibiting their dogs.

Imported Affenpinschers continued to make their mark into the 1960s. Mrs. Lester H. Tillman, Jr. of Oyster Bay, New York, owned and exhibited the top-winning Affenpinscher of 1963, Ch. Babs von Reburg. This little dog came from Austria.

A number of midwestern breeders helped to advance the breed during the 1960s and '70s. Jean and Bill Becker, from Decatur, Illinois, starting with the Walhof lines, bred and exhibited many fine Affenpinschers under the Je-Bil

kennel name. The Kauffmanns owned and exhibited Ch. Je-Bil's Yogi Bear, who was one of that era's top show dogs.

The Reverend Clyde Zarski and his Apache kennels from Rhinelander, Wisconsin combined the Walhof and Aff-Airn lines to produce a number of fine champions. Mrs. Lois Wolf (McManus) White, now a dog show judge living in California, handled dogs for and co-owned dogs with Rev. Zarski. One of these dogs of note was top-winning Ch. Apache Cricket Again. Mrs. White also bred a few litters and has been active with the development of the AKC Affenpinscher breed video and the breed standard. In the 1970s Kay Wurtz, also from Wisconsin, under the King's Royal name, continued with the Apache lines and bred and showed Affens until the late '80s.

It seems that the 1960s brought much enthusiasm, interest and controversy to the breed. Breeders gathered to form a club but soon there were arguments over the standard and, specifically, over the height of the Affenpinscher. Some wanted the breed to remain at 10.25 inches. Others felt that the dogs would be sounder and easier to breed if they were a bit larger. This battle became heated and caused a split in the club, with one faction forming the American Affenpinscher Association and the other the Affenpinscher Club of

HAVE YOU HEARD?
Here an unsubstantiated story needs to be related. The rumor is that during the mid-1950s a breeder, who was a scientist and concerned with the fragileness and light bones in the breed at that time, found a small black undershot Miniature Schnauzer female. He surreptitiously included her into the breeding program of his well-known Affenpinscher kennel. The sources for this information explained that many of the young Affens at the time were breaking their legs and lacked the necessary bone density. This "out-cross" was intended to rectify this problem. Some of these offspring went to the Midwest, as well as to several breeders in the East. It was felt that this infusion of new genes did improve the situation. Some of the larger-sized, longer-muzzled Affenpinschers can be traced back to this experiment.

America. With time and civility the fancy joined together again as the Affenpinscher Club of America, which still exists but is still often embroiled in controversy.

The Affenpinscher, as a respected show dog with consistent group placements, started to make its mark in the mid-1970s. More professional handlers and enthusiastic breeder-exhibitors got involved. The overall quality and showmanship in the breed improved. A more refined and sculptured appearance for the show ring developed. The judges took note and more and more Affenpinschers began placing and winning in the toy ring. However, what the appropriate look is or how much grooming is right for the breed added to the controversy.

THE MODERN ERA

Jerry Zalon, who started with the Walhof kennels in the 1950s, founded the Eblon kennels in New York City in the '70s. He specialized in producing the various colors of the breed. His breeding program continued into the '80s with the help of Osmin and Marjorie Montjovier, whose Osmar kennel name is behind many of the dogs in Canada and the US. Their Am. and Can. Ch. Eblon Seal Noir was the top-winning Affenpinscher in 1976. This dog was often shown by Mrs. Jane Forsyth. During the late '60s Mr. Zalon and Ms. Montjovier began writing an Affenpinscher periodical named *Monkey Shines.* This publication continued for only a short time, but it reflected the interest and enthusiasm for the breed.

In Canada, during the 1970s and '80s, Vicki Garrett-Knill started with the Osmar Affens and added the Hilane bloodlines to produce both fine show and obedience dogs. Her kennel name was Wicksteed. One of her breeding, which was owned by the author, Ch. Wicksteed's Red Capuchin, was one of the top-producing dams, with seven champions. She was out of Can. Ch.

Wicksteed's Marmoset Rouge bred to Ch. Sharpette's Tiny Tim. Another of her contributions was in the red and wild boar or belge colors. These colored specimens were of excellent type. Vicki and Carl Knill and their family have moved to Georgia and are no longer active in the breed. Marjorie and David Reynolds continue with these lines in Canada under the prefix Reyson. A red female out of Ch. FMK's Zulu of Hilane and Wick-steed's Tekahionwake, Ch. Reyson's Sunshine Too V Hilane is behind some important and successful show dogs.

In the mid-1960s Mrs. Lillian Brandi, from Hackettstown, New Jersey, began with Affenpinschers from the Walhof kennels and Brandicreek dogs bred by Helen Barbeau. Mrs. Brandi showed her Ch. Walhof Blackberry Brandi to prestigious wins in 1967 and '68. She was credited with changing the grooming style of the show Affen-pinscher by neatening and shaping the outline and reducing the amount of body coat. This new image for the breed gained her notice. Of course controversy ensued and the debate over what is the correct "look" for the breed continues today. Her breeding program continued into the 1980s with a dog that she bred, Ch. Brandicreek Frisky Whisky, who did some nice winning. Frisky Whisky was owned and handled by Howard and Joyce Stadele of

A red champion, Ch. Reyson's Sunshine Too V Hilane, bred by Marjorie Reynolds, has produced many important Affenpinschers.

Middlesex, New Jersey.

Mrs. Emily Kinsley of Easton, Pennsylvania was another who started her breeding program with dogs from the Harringtons. On June 25, 1966, *This Week,* the Sunday newspaper supplement, had a photo of Mrs. Kinsley's puppy, Aff-Airn A Go Go Kins, on its cover. This gave the breed some much-needed publicity. The top-winning Affen-pinscher for 1966, owned by Mrs. Kinsley, was Ch. Aff-Airn Wee Winnie Winkie, who also came from

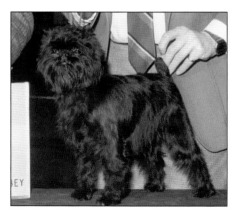

Ch. FMK's Zulu of Hilane is the sire of Ch. Reyson's Sunshine Too V Hilane (shown above).

Ch. Hilane's Lonesome Cowboy, bred by William Beskie and owner Jerome Cushman, became the fourth Affen to win an all-breed Best in Show. He is currently the top sire in the breed.

Canada. Later, in 1991, Chewy's and Ch. Hilane's Lonesome Cowboy's son Am. and Can. Ch. Ceterra's Rock-N-Robbie won a US national specialty and an American all-breed Best in Show. Robbie was shown by Mrs. Delores Burkholder, who is at the time of this writing an AKC dog show representative. More recently Robbie's son Can. Ch. Ceterra's Billy the Kid joined his grandmother to be the second Affenpinscher to win a Canadian all-breed Best in Show. Another of Rock-N-Robbie's sons, Ch. Ceterra's Little Black Sambo, out of Ch. Aff-Kin's Kischia Frolics, is the sire of several of the top show dogs today. Lorna Spratt and Sherry Galagan continue to breed and exhibit in Canada.

Starting with the Aff-Kin's Affens, Sue and Don Spahr of Scottsdale, Arizona developed the Su-Dawn line. Their most famous dog was multiple Best in Show and

Am. and Can. Ch. Ceterra's Rock-N-Robbie, a national specialty and Best in Show winner.

the Harringtons. Winkie had her photo in *National Geographic.* This bitch won Best of Breed at the Inter-national Dog Show over an entry of 21, the largest entry for the breed at that time. She was also the second owner-handled Affen to place first in the Toy Group. For the next 25 years Mrs. Kinsley's Aff-Kin's line produced many champions and had a positive impact on the breed. Her Can. Ch. Aff-Kin's Licorice Chewy, owned by Mrs. Lorna (Thompson) Spratt of Winnipeg, Manitoba, Canada, became the first Affenpin-scher to win Best in Show in

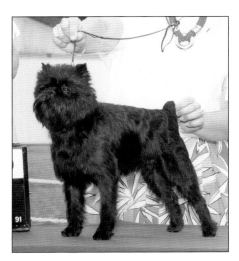

national specialty winner in 1992, Ch. Su-Dawn's Pee Wee Herman. This great show dog did much for the breed, especially in the West during the early '90s. Pee Wee's dam was Ch. Su-Dawn's Affins Krystal, bred by Emily Kinsley. She became a top producer with eight champions from another of their fine dogs, Ch. Su-Dawn's Where Thear's Smoke. Utilizing the Su-Dawn lines, Judith Benjamin also bred Affenpinschers in the Southwest. She owned Ch. Subira's Whoopie Goldberg, who did very well in the show ring in the early '90s.

Another important early breeder, Lucille E. Meystedt, who came from Missouri and later moved to Texas, began in Affenpinschers in 1962. Starting with a dog bred by the Kauffmanns named Walhof Hi Quotation and females from Cassel Hills kennels, who also go back to Walhof lines, she kept the breed going in the southern and western parts of the United States through the 1980s. In 1967 she brought in a dog from Germany. This male, Ch. Vinzenz v Greifensee, was the most titled Affenpinscher in the history of the breed. He had his International, German, American, Canadian, Mexican and Colombian championships. Another of her breeding, Ch. Balu's Arkady Herzchen Katze, who was called "Sugar," became the fifth Affenpinscher to earn an all-breed Best in Show. Mary and Bill Wasson and George and Phyllis Willis of

The most famous dog from Su-Dawn Affens is multiple Best in Show and national specialty winner Ch. Su-Dawn's Pee Wee Herman, owned by Don and Sue Spahr. Pee Wee did much for the breed in the West during the 1990s.

Texas owned Sugar.

Mrs. Meystedt's Balu kennels continued until her death in 1991. In almost 30 years in the breed she had a major influence on the Affenpinscher not only with her breeding program but also through her writings in the magazine *Popular Dogs* and as an AKC dog show judge. She

Ch. Balu's Arkady Herzchen Katze, "Sugar," bred by Lucille E. Meystedt and owned by Mary and Bill Wasson and George and Phyllis Willis, became the fifth Affenpinscher to win an all-breed BIS.

exported dogs to England, Ireland, Australia and Germany. Lucille Meystedt showed and finished one of the first Affenpinschers with natural ears.

Another Texas exhibitor and breeder is Elizabeth Muir-Chamberlain who began with dogs from George and Phyllis Willis. Soon she produced Am., Mex., World and Int. Ch. Periwinkle Godzilla, whose sire and dam are Ch. Cetera's Little Black Sambo and Ch. Tajar's Midnight Munchkin. Godzilla did well in the show ring and produced several of today's top show dogs. These include Ch. Yarrow's Mighty Joe Young, bred by Beth Sweigart, Letisha Wubbel and Doris Tolone and owned by Dr. and Mrs. William Truesdale, and Ch. Hilane's Harry Potter, the top-winning Affenpinscher in Canada, owned by Sandra Lex.

In New Mexico, Patricia Bouldin continues with the Balu bloodlines and added King's Royal dogs from the late Kay Wurtz. Bouldin's Tajar Affenpinschers have had an impact on England as well as America. Barbara and Jenna Gresser in Arizona have used and exhibited the Tajar dogs and dogs from Marilyn Holt in Oregon to develop their breeding and exhibiting program under the name Black Forest. Among their important dogs is Ch. Black Forest Cookie Monster.

THE HAWAIIAN IMPACT
The tidal-wave event in the modern history of the Affenpinscher was the birth of the famous Hawaiian litter. This occurred when Ellen and Gil Stoewsand, from Geneva, New York, bought a male whose name was Deer Run Goblin Del Cocagi from Tobin Jackson. After completing

From the famous Hawaiian five came these two top winners: Ch. El Cocagi Eli Eli Wahine, "Posey," (left) and Ch. El Cocagi Kamehameha, "Bear" (right), bred by Ellen and Gil Stoewsand.

Goblin's championship, Mrs. Stoewsand searched for several years before she managed to obtain a female from Lucille Meystedt, Ch. Balu's Schwartz Diamant. Unexpectedly the Stoewsands received a six-month appointment to go to the University of Hawaii. Dr. Gil Stoewsand is a researcher for Cornell University. A few days into the new year of 1976, Gil, Ellen and their two daughters, Corrine and Cathy, with their two Affens landed in Honolulu. Because Hawaii is rabies free, the dogs had to remain in quarantine for four months. In February of 1976, while in quarantine, a litter of six puppies was delivered by C-section from Ch. Balu's Schwartz Diamant, who was called "Dema." Dr. and Mrs. Stoewsand had high praise for the concern and care their dogs received while in quarantine. They were allowed to visit them daily and the facilities were excellent. This information is included here to allay some of the fears associated with putting dogs into quarantine, as is necessary in England, parts of Europe and many of the rabies-free islands. Dogs, from most reports, come out of the experience in good condition and well adjusted.

Of these six puppies out of Goblin and Dema, one did not survive the first week. Another male was very weak and lived only through the heroic efforts of the Stoewsands' youngest daughter, Cathy, and was later kept at their

Here's Ch. El Cocagi's Panda Bear, an important sire in the breed.

home as a pet. A third male was sold to a woman in Hawaii who later took the dog back to Germany. Of the four brought back to the mainland, two were kept and shown by Mrs. Stoewsand, Ch. El Cocagi Alii, whose name means "Royalty," and Ch. El Cocagi Eli Eli Wahine, which means "Black Girl" in Hawaiian. Alii was called "Taz" and was later sold to Julianna Bitter in California. "Posey," which was Eli Eli Wahine's call name, had a prestigious show career, starting with winning Best of Breed at the Affenpinscher Club of America's first specialty match in 1976. She was even more influential as a top-producing female.

The fourth puppy was a male bought by professional handler Robert Sharp for his daughter Jennifer. This dog was named Ch. El Cocagi Kamehameha (named for the last king of Hawaii) and called "Bear." He was the top-winning Affenpinscher for several years. On

Ch. Balu's Schwartz Zucker Fuss, bred by Lucille Meystedt.

June 11, 1978, Bear became the first Affenpinscher to receive an all-breed Best in Show, under judge Robert Wills at the Tonawanda Valley Kennel Club in upstate New York. In 1980 he won Best of Breed at the first officially supported entry for Affenpinschers. Champion El Cocagi Kamehameha was a wonderful show dog and attracted many enthusiasts to the breed.

Mr. Sharp's assistant at the time, who conditioned, groomed and later owned Bear, was Bonnie (Hawkins) Sellner. She has had a long and continuing association with the breed as a handler, owner and breeder. Her kennel name is Wyn Willow. Several dogs from her breeding out of Kamehameha or his offspring have made an impact on the breed. Giancarlo Volante, from California, showed a triple Kamehameha great-grandson, Ch. Puff Von Apache Rauchen, who became

the third Affenpinscher to win an all-breed Best in Show. He repeated this feat with several more Bests, including two in Mexico.

The second all-breed Best in Show winning Affenpinscher, and first female to do so, was Ch. Christina v. Silber Wald, owned by Jack and Joann Beutel of Portland, Oregon and handled by Paul and Pauline Booher. Because there were so few Affenpinschers in the area where "Chrissy" lived and was shown, she had to finish her championship by winning the Toy Group. Margret Lewis of Tuxedo, New York bred Chrissy. Mrs. Lewis came from Germany and imported her original

AFFEN SMOKE IN OBEDIENCE

In 1980 there was another first for the Affenpinscher breed. Vicki Hart Schierer's Ch. Me Own T G's Smoke Signal became the first conformation champion and Utility Dog obedience title winner. Theresa Battle bred "Smokey." His remarkable achievement was accomplished in just nine shows. There have been a large number of obedience title winners, and several breeders work hard in this ring with great success. Terry Graham, Lois Brockson, Birdee Hills, Peggy Mershon, Mae Aspinall Dell, Barbara Swisher, Dr. Alice Schotlenstein, and Gilly Rank have been leaders for the breed in obedience training and work in agility as well. The Affenpinscher is very intelligent and loves to work if you begin training early on.

breeding stock from there. Chrissy's sire was Ch. Von Tiki's My Pal Joey and her dam was Primrose v. Silber Wald. Linda and Dorothy Strydio, who bred and exhibited a number of Affens during the 1970 and '80s, bred the sire.

During the 1980s the Stoewsands continued the El Cocagi line and bred the top show dogs as well as top producers. Most of the top-winning Affenpinschers in the show ring during the 1980s and '90s had one or more of the three champions from that Hawaiian litter in their pedigrees. These three dogs significantly changed the quality and type of the breed all over the world. Another of the notable dogs was Ch. El Cocagi Black Baron, who had been purchased and shown by Quentin and Blanche Roberts from California. They made him one of the top show dogs in the early '80s.

Marjorie and David Saylor, who had finished a number of Deer Run Affens, bought Ch. El Cocagi Vampira who was out of Ch. Balu's Schwartz Zucker and El Cocagi Scarlet O'Hare. She became a top producer with nine champions. She was bred to the Saylors' little red dog, Ch. Deer Run's Eric the Red. The Saylors' Mountain View Affenpinschers are behind a number of fine red and black Affens.

One of Vampira's sons by Ch. Flo-Star's Little Tiam, Ch. El Cocagi Wilhelm, went to England, where he joined some other of the Flo-Star Affens at Wendy Boorer's Furstin

One of the Hilane Affens added to the breeding program of Patricia and Dr. Christine Dresser, this is Ch. Hilane's Dress Circle Sunray, the black and tan sire of Ch. Dress Circle Good Grrief.

kennels. Wilhelm and a grandson out of Ch. Hilane's Lonesome Cowboy have contributed greatly to the Affenpinschers in the UK. Mrs. Rita Turner, whose kennel name is Gerbrae, and the late Mrs. Pat Patchen, whose prefix was Zipaty, imported five American Affenpinschers. These dogs from Hilane and Tajar added to Balu, Flo-Star, Vroni Kleine and El Cocagi lines comprise the majority of the American influence in England. According to *The*

Ch. Dress Circle Good Grrief, bred by Patricia and Dr. Christine Dresser, won ten all-breed Bests in Show, expertly handled by Tom Glassford.

DETROIT KENNEL CLUB MARCH 9 1980

TOY GROUP

JUDGE MR MAXWELL RIDDLE

First Fifty Affenpinscher Champions, compiled by Dr. M. Brown and Mrs. S. Pirrie, every current-day chanpion goes back to these lines.

FURTHER WAVES OF SUCCESS

Because of the success of the El Cocagi Affenpinschers, more of the established kennels began to share their bloodlines more readily. Aff-Kins, Balu and Flo-Star kennels, with a number of new enthusiasts, eagerly crossed out to one another's stock and improved on each of their lines. Behind all of the top contemporary show dogs one will find these four kennel names.

Another of the modern influential breeding programs is this author's own Hilane kennels. Starting with a Kamehameha son, Ch. Sharpette's Tiny Tim, and a female from the Stoewsands, Ch. El Cocagi Wunder Dame v. Hilane, the Hilane Affenpinschers are included in many breeding programs in North America, England, Australia, France, Sweden, Poland and Finland.

Two females from Tiny Tim and Wunder Dame won Toy Groups in the early 1980s. One of these daughters was Ch. Hilane Dress Circle Best Bet, owned and exhibited by Patricia Dresser and her daughter Dr. Christine Dresser of Medina, Ohio. Best Bet won the Toy Group from the Puppy Class at the prestigious Detroit Kennel Club Dog Show in 1980. The Dressers added several more Hilane Affens to their kennel. A black and tan, Ch. Hilane's Dress Circle Sunray, out of Lonesome Cowboy, sired one of the top all-breed Best in Show-winning dogs, Ch. Dress Circle Good Grrief. This wonderful show dog won ten all-breed BISs handled by the well-known dog aficionado and AKC dog show official Tom Glassford. In 1989 Ch. Dress Circle Grrease Monkey, co-owned and shown by Dani Rosenberry, won the national specialty under judge James Cavallaro. Another of their breeding, Ch. Dress Circle Grrilla, owned by Connie and Marvin Clapp, won an all-breed Best in Show. Connie Clapp has been active in the breed club and is an AKC judge.

The winner of the first two AKC-licensed national Affenpinscher specialties in 1986 and 1987, the fourth Affen to win an all-breed Best in Show and, to date, all-time top-producing sire is Ch. Hilane's Lonesome Cowboy, bred, owned and shown by Jerome Cushman. His progeny continue to be the top-winning and top-producing Affenpinschers in North America and England. Cowboy's sire was Ch. El Cocagi's Wilhelm. Among the other notable Hilane Affenpinschers are Ch. Hilane's Lili Marlene, Cowboy's dam, who won Best of Breed at a supported entry under the late judge Herr Hans Holler, who at the time was president of the German PSK (Pinscher Schnauzer Club), and Ch. Hilane's I'll Be Jiggered, who was a top winner and supported-entry breed winner under Edith Nash Hellerman in 1981. Both Lili and Jiggers were co-owned by William

LEFT: National specialty winner Ch. Dress Circle Grrease Monkey, co-owned and shown by Dani Rosenberry. RIGHT: All-breed BIS winner Ch. Dress Circle Grrilla, owned by Connie and Marvin Clapp.

Ch. Hilane's I'll Be Jiggered, co-owned by William Beskie and Bonnie (Beskie) Ross, produced a number of top sires for the breed.

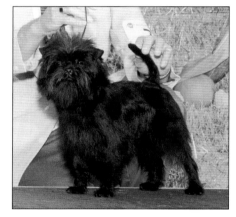

Ch. Hilane's Reggie White, owned by Jerome Cushman.

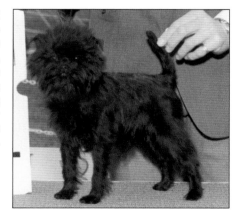

Bred, owned and handled by author Jerome Cushman, Ch. Hilane's Marlane was the first group-placing Affenpinscher with natural ears and tail.

Beskie and Bonnie Sue (Beskie) Ross. Bonnie Sue Ross was an ardent Affenpinscher enthusiast and worked as the secretary for the Affenpinscher Club of America when the AKC first formally recognized this club and when the first revised breed standard was accepted in 1990. Jiggers, bred to Ch. El Cocagi's Panda Bear, produced some important males who have contributed greatly to the breed. One of them was Ch. Hilane's Oberon of Wicksteed, owned by Vicki Garrett-Knill.

Another important Affen was Ch. Hilane's Procyon, owned by Peter Fine and Ramona Martinez Fine. This dog, called "Al," along with Lonesome Cowboy's son Ch. Hilane's Alpha Centauri, became the foundation sires for the Osgood Farm's Affenpinschers. Their first female was Ch. Wyn Willow Sirius from Bonnie Sellner. The most notable offspring of Ch. Hilane's Alpha Centauri and Ch. Wyn Willow Sirius was the multiple Best in Show-winning Ch. Osgood Farm's Bull Market. "Bully" was shown by both Ramona Fine and Maripi Wooldridge and won the 1990 national specialty. He was the sire of several champions including the top-winning show dogs, Ch. Osgood Farm's Mighty Mouse. Dr. and Mrs. Brian Shack from Long Island, New York owned "Mouse." This specialty and multiple BIS winner was shown first by Robert Fisher and later by the famous dog handler Peter Green. Mouse placed twice in the Toy Group at the prestigious Westminster Dog Show. He has gone on to produce several champions. Ch. Terian's Black Storm Rising is one of special note. The Shacks' dogs included some of Nancy Bryant's Rosehill females in their Terian breeding program. Dr. Shack passed away in 2004.

In 1988 the first female to win a national Affenpinscher specialty was Ch. Ken-Jo's Little Affen Annie, bred by Ken and Josephine Harkins and owned by Barbara Sayres. This granddaughter of both Kamehameha and of top-producing Ch. El Cocagi's Vampira was Mrs. Sayres's first Affenpinscher. Soon Barbara and her husband Richard, who was from a well-known dog-showing family that specialized in Kerry Blue Terriers, became very involved with the breed. They bred Annie to Ch. Hilane's Lonesome Cowboy, which was the start of the Gibbs Pond Affenpinschers. Later, the Sayreses purchased a female from Vicki Garrett-Knill, Ch. Wicksteed Cuddler of Gibbs Pond. Their Gibbs Pond kennel moved from Long Island to Maryland and later to Florida, where the Sayreses have retired from showing.

Ken and Josephine Harkins, also from Long Island, started their Affen program with the Mountain View dogs acquired from Dave and Marjorie Saylor. The Harkinses have produced some very fine black and red Affenpinschers including Ch.

In 1988 Ch. Ken-Jo's Little Affen Annie became the first female to win the national specialty. She was owned by Barbara A. Sayres of the Gibbs Pond kennels and bred by Ken and Josephine M. Harkins.

Ken-Jo's Little Affen Annie's red litter sister, Ch. Ken-Jo Ginger Schnapps.

In Connecticut Sharon and Richard Strempski, long-time breeders and founding members of the Affenpinscher Club of America, have their Vroni Kleine kennel. They began with the Aff-Kins lines along with dogs imported from Germany. Later they exported to Germany and England. Sharon has judged Affens in the US and England.

In New Hampshire Nancy E. Holmes's FMK lines produced World and Am. Ch. FMK's Zulu of Hilane, who was number-one Affenpinscher in 1989. He was sold to fanciers in Sweden and later went to new owners in New Zealand. The "Flying Monkey Kennel" (hence FMK) now has added some German lines to the breeding program and has exported a number of dogs to Europe.

Nancy Baybutt's Sienna Gold kennel in Massachusetts, using Flo-Star, Doch's, Terian and Hilane lines, has been producing some excellent Affenpinschers for a number of years.

With the passing of Flo Strohmaier in October 2005, an over 50-year breeding program came to an end. However, Mary Ann and Shirley Welch in Santa Paula, California are continuing the Flo-Star lines and have shown and finished a large number of the Flo-Star dogs in recent years.

IMPORTANT AFFENPINSCHERS OF THE MODERN ERA

Ch. Hilane's Solar Eclipse was born May 9, 1991 and died September 11, 2004. Solar was bred and owned by Jerome Cushman and Frederick

Ch. Yarrow's Super Nova, pictured winning the Group at Westminster in 2002. Owned by Dr. and Mrs. William Truesdale, "Cosmos" was the first Affenpinscher to accomplish this feat. Cosmos was bred by Beth K. Sweigart and Letisha Wubbel.

Nuernberg. Solar was one of three puppies in the litter. His rather unique color inspired his name. On his neck, shoulders and flanks he had a dark red undercoat with a black overlay of hard coat. Many times he has thrown this characteristic coat color. He was Winners Dog under judge Sari Brewster Tietjen at the national specialty in 1992.

His brother Ch. Hilane's Seth Thomas, owned by Carolyn (Garrity) Hamilton, won the national specialty in 1993 under judge Lois Wolf White. His sister Ch. Hilane's Au Naturel was the first all-natural Affenpinscher to earn an AKC championship.

At about the age of two-and-a-half, Solar showed signs of stiffness and the veterinarian reported he had been infected with Lyme's disease, which left him with severe arthritis. He was a stoic little dog who enjoyed life with only minor accommodations.

Though he was not used a lot for breeding, he has produced some great dogs. His offspring include national specialty winners Ch. Hilane's Harpagon, later owned by Shirley Howard and Jim and Kathy Herman, Ch. Yarrow's Lucy in the Sky (Moraina), owned by Jackie Stacy and Ch. Yarrow's Super Nova (Cosmos), owned by Dr. and Mrs. William Truesdale.

"Moraina" and "Cosmos" hold the records for most Best in Show wins for their sex in the breed. Cosmos also was the top toy and

One of Mighty Joe Young's kids, Ch. Yarrow's Thrill Monkey, owned by Dr. and Mrs. William Truesdale and bred by Beth K. Sweigart and Letisha Wubbel.

number-five top-winning all-breed show dog for 2001. Ranked as the number-eight all-time top-winning toy dog, he was the first Affenpinscher to win the Toy Group at the Westminster Kennel Club Dog Show. A brother of Cosmos is multiple group winner and top producer Ch. Yarrow's Over The Moon. His sister is Ch. Kyleakin Maid At Yarrow, who has produced several top-winning champions. Ch. Yarrow's Lucy in the Sky's littermate is Ch. Yarrow's Rocketman, who lives with Sharon Sapp in Georgia, and he too has sired some nice dogs.

Other of Solar's sons who have done well in the show ring is Ch. Tamarin Trevor, owned by David and Pamela Peat. Trevor's brother Ch. Tamarin Tanz, owned by Joseph Reinisch, also has been a fine show dog.

Another son, Ch. Hilane's The Sun Also Rises, owned and exhibited by Rebecca Brandon and

An English import bred by Rita Turner, Ch. Gerbraes Maid In Splendour, or "Doris," is the dam of Cosmos and is related to most of today's top Affens. Owners, Beth K. Sweigart and Letisha Wubbel.

Babettta P. Veater in Alaska, has won several groups and a Best in Show. His littermate Ch. Hilane Spring's Awakening has sired a number of fine champions including Ch. Hilane's Just Look At Me, owned by Sandra Lex from Canada, and Ch. Hi-Tech Girlrilla Of My Dream, owned by Beth Sweigart and Letisha Wubbel. Two of Solar's granddaughters, Ch. Hilane's Betty Boop and Ch. Hilane's Loose Cannon, also are group winners.

Solar also sired some quality belge bitches, including Ch. Hilane's Molley Sugden, who has produced three champions for her owner Mavis Weatherwax of California, and Ch. Hilane's Present, owned by Jerome Cushman. Solar sired Ch. Hilane's Marlane, the first group-placing Affenpinscher with natural ears and tail.

While visiting Crufts Dog Show in England Beth Sweigart and Peter Green spotted a young female Affenpinscher owned by Rita Turner. They purchased her and brought her back to show and add to their breeding program. She finished her championship fast and won some large breed competitions. She is the dam and grand-dam of many of today's top-winning Affenpinschers. Her name is Ch. Gerbraes Maid In Splendour, whose call name is "Doris," and she is owned by Beth Sweigart and Letisha Wubbel. Her littermate Ch. Gerbraes Maid in Heaven at Zipaty, owned by the late Pat Patchen, was a top show bitch in England.

Bred to Solar, Doris produced other important Affens in addition to Cosmos and Moraina. These include Ch. Yarrow's Over The

Ch. Hilane's Lonesome Cowboy, winning Best in Show with owner/handler Jerome Cushman.

Moon and Ch. Kyleakin Maid At Yarrow. Doris also has more champions bred to other males. Ch. Yarrow's Mighty Joe Young won the specialty in 2004. Two more fine champions who are winning Bests are Ch. Bukany Streakmeister Tamarin and Ch. Yarrow's Action Jackson.

After Moraina earned her championship, Beth Sweigart gave her to Jackie and Terry Stacy, who have used her to start their Tamarin lines. Doris's other daughter, Ch. Kyleakin Maid At Yarrow, was also given to the Stacys and Doris Tolone of Calkerry Affenpinschers. These two foundation bitches along with Ch. Periwinkle En-La Ms. Munster, bred by Elizabeth Muir-Chamberlain, were the source for the Affenpinschers at Tamarin and Calkerry. These bitches were bred to Hilane, Periwinkle, Doch's and Ceterra males to produce some highly campaigned Affenpinschers. Doris Tolone's Ch. Tamarin Talullah (out of Ch. Periwinkle Godzilla and Ch. Kyleakin Maid At Yarrow) won the national specialty in 2001. Ch. Ceterra's Little Black Sambo, bred to Ch. Tamarin Tulip, produced Ch. Tamarin Travis (2002 and 2003

Son of Godzilla, here's top-winning Ch. Yarrow's Mighty Joe Young, bred by Beth K. Sweigart, Letisha Wubbel and Doris Tolone and owned by Dr. and Mrs. William Truesdale.

national specialty winner) and Ch. Tamarin Tip-Off (2005 national specialty winner).

The future for the Affenpinscher looks bright. More good champions are placing in and winning Groups across North America. Let's hope that the breed does not become too popular and that the new breeders stay focused on producing healthy, happy and well-adjusted dogs who fulfill the function of the fun-loving family pet.

CHARACTERISTICS OF THE

AFFENPINSCHER

By Jerome Cushman and Jo Ann White

This Affenpinscher uses his agile front limbs to give his Bedlington Terrier friend a hug.

"Look at that scruffy little dog! Isn't that an adorable face?"

"That's so ugly, it's cute. What kind of dog is that?"

"Look at him prancing around, just like a little old man!"

People who own, exhibit and breed the Affenpinscher hear these kinds of comments all the time. This relatively uncommon, but old, breed is slowly gaining respect by the dog fancy and the public as well. One experienced dog enthusiast, after living with and showing his first Affenpinscher, was heard to say, "This breed is the best-kept secret in the dog world, and I hope it stays that way." The Affenpinscher has a small but loyal following in North America and Europe. Its history and development as a respected member of the canine community is an interesting but unfamiliar story.

WHAT IS THE AFFENPINSCHER?

This German tot is a clever, sturdy little dog who loves to frolic with his master in almost any kind of environment. The Affen, which is the nickname that many friends of the breed use, adapts well to a variety of living arrangements, from small city apartments to lavish homes with acres of land in which to romp. The word *Affen*, in the German language, means to ape or to mock. From this it came to mean monkey-like behavior or appearance. Therefore, the name is often translated as "monkey terrier." Interestingly, both its looks and actions are reflected in this name. The viewer quickly gets a decidedly "simian" impression from his scruffy whiskers and eyebrows, which frame the full, dark and intense eyes. This image is reinforced by an Affen's willingness to walk or hop on his hind legs and bat the air with his front paws in a comical dance. The inquisitive tilting head and the devilish stare, followed by a sudden dashing off in a playful gallop, can't help but bring a smile to an observer's face. Because of the penetrating stare and these mischievous antics, the breed is called the "Diablotin Moustachu" or the "mustached little devil" in France. The distinctive round head with full, dark eyes, short muzzle, slightly undershot lower teeth, pouting mouth and hard shaggy coat are important characteristics for the typical "monkey-like terrier."

The Affenpinscher is a toy breed ranging in height from 9 to 12 inches at the shoulder, ideally 10.25 inches. The body is moderately thick and square. The rib cage is generally more egg-shaped than barrel-shaped. The mature dog will weigh between 7 and 12 pounds. The back is short and level. The lengths of the upper and lower front legs are equal, and the legs are straight, not bowed or out at the elbows. The rear legs are straight, not cow-hocked, with moderate angulation. One health problem that affects many toy breeds is the luxation of the patella or the slipping of the kneecaps. This is a concern for some Affenpinscher breeders, and one needs to be aware that lameness in the rear legs may occur as a result of this genetic weakness.

In North America the colors of the coat include black, black and tan, gray, red, wild boar or belge, and all of these colors may have various shadings from light tan to dark red. The lighter-colored dogs may have black or dark gray masks. Generally, there are more black Affenpinschers than any other color. These black dogs often develop mixtures of white, reddish brown or gray hairs in their adult coats.

The coat quality has varying degrees of coarseness, depending upon the type of hair, its color and its care. Some coats are of a

LOOKS LIKE A MONKEY...

The Affenpinscher uses his front paws with great dexterity, much like a monkey. He may hold his toys in his paws, use his paws to hold down another dog or put his paws around his owner's neck. He also uses his paws to climb, and some Affenpinschers have been known to easily scale ladders.

very hard texture, without much undercoat and with sparse furnishings. Some may have an abundance of undercoat and thick furnishings on the legs and head. Correct grooming and coat care will keep each of the extremes more suitable for the breed. Preference is for the hard coat with an undercoat that allows for full furnishings on the head and legs.

The ears, which are set high, may be cropped to a point or left natural. The natural or uncropped ears usually tip forward but may also stand up erect. The tail can be docked or left long or natural. The docked tail on an adult is about 1–2 inches long, set and carried high. The undocked tail is carried curved, gaily up over the

TERRIER ON DUTY
The Affenpinscher was originally bred to catch rats. This means that it does not share its home well with hamsters, gerbils or other rodent or rodent-like small pets. Regardless of how well behaved your pet may be, there are times when instinct takes over!

back when the dog is moving or is happy and attentive. The undocked and uncropped Affenpinscher presents a different overall image of the breed, but it should not be penalized in the show ring. In most of Europe the breed is required to be natural.

Today more than three-quarters of the Affenpinschers in America have natural or uncropped ears. Still, in the US and Canada one will see the majority of Affenpinschers in the show ring with docked tails. Even so, one of the breed's top bitches has both natural ears and tail. Ch. Yarrow's Lucy in the Sky, "Moraina," as she is called, has a famous brother with natural ears (but a docked tail). He is "Cosmos," the number-one Affenpinscher, formally Ch. Yarrow's Super Nova. The all-natural Affenpinscher is steadily gaining popularity in America. Large or small, black or red, cropped and docked or natural, the Affenpinscher is a distinct and delightful breed.

Showing properly cropped and high-set ears, this red Affenpinscher captures the breed's monkey-like expression and ineffable appeal.

FUNCTION AND TEMPERAMENT

The original function of the breed was that of a rodent killer in the kitchens, barns, stables and granaries. Some report that the Affen was used to flush out small game, also. Over the past three centuries the Affenpinscher has become a loved family companion who is willing to be dressed up in doll clothes by the young girls and pushed around in a baby carriage. But the dog is also willing to roughhouse in the yard or go chasing a ball with the boys. The breed's flexible front quarters allow the playful pet to quickly pivot, scoop up a ball and literally toss it toward his master. Going for long walks or sitting on the sofa watching TV with the family, the Affenpinscher adapts and thrives with all kinds of human interaction. However, children under four years old or

The Affenpinscher's compact size and endearing personality make it hard to stop at owning just one. This is Mrs. Margaret Boulcott from Scotland with a quartet of Affens, two of which are Flo-Star imports.

older children who do not respect the dog's need for space and quiet time should not have an Affenpinscher. As with any small dog, uncontrolled little people can appear to be the enemy. Extra care should be taken to introduce the puppy into a family with young children.

Generally, this breed is a wonderful companion. It travels well and can accompany the family almost anywhere and by almost any means of transportation. In an adequately sized dog crate, a soft-sided doggie carrying case with a net covered opening, or any small pet-carrying case, as long as his master or mistress is near, the Affen makes a quiet and

TONGUE-IN-CHEEK TRAINING

When training an Affenpinscher for obedience or agility, you must make the training seem like play. This is a highly intelligent breed that rebels at harsh training methods—but that's part of what makes training an Affenpinscher both fun and frustrating. As one writer said, "If you own a dog that looks and acts like a monkey, you better have a sense of humor."

easy traveling companion.

The Affenpinscher makes an alert, intelligent and amusing pet. His personality well suits his whimsical, monkey-like appearance and the twinkle in his eyes. Imagine, if you will, a dog that loves to throw and chase his own toys, using his front paws as hands. If you laugh at his antics, your Affenpinscher will perform even more enthusiastically for your entertainment. It is quite common for him to accompany his play with a great deal of enthusiastic racing around and barking, although retrieving is not something that generally comes naturally. One of the funniest

A natural performer, the Affenpinscher brings both fun and challenges to your training sessions with his comical antics.

things we've ever observed was an Affenpinscher attacking a wind-up stuffed dog that walked, barked and flipped over. With this in mind, child's toys are best kept out of the dog's reach, and all of the Affen's toys should be checked carefully for suitability. Toys with small parts or materials inside that could injure the dog if ingested should be avoided or allowed only with supervision.

Another characteristic of this breed is its independence, which sometimes verges on aloofness. The Affenpinscher has a great sense of its own self-importance, which is comical in a breed so small and endearingly bedraggled.

This delightful little creature also makes an excellent watchdog, barking vociferously as his first line of defense if he feels his territory is being invaded (even by the postman). Originally bred to guard his domain from intruders, be they rodent, canine or human, an Affenpinscher will still defend his property (including his owners) fearlessly.

It is likely that the Affen will bond most closely to one member of your family. While he is generally a quiet and affectionate companion, he is likely to become extremely excited and aggressive if he perceives that he or his owners are being attacked. This means that you should be careful when introducing your pet to visitors, and make sure that he understands that they are welcome in his home. Speak to your dog softly and soothingly, and allow him to approach your visitors when he is ready, rather than forcing their attentions on him. He may feel insecure or become frightened if a stranger bends down to pet him. It is also not a good idea for a stranger to stare directly into your Affen's eyes, as he may interpret this as a challenge.

Although Affens do have a terrier-like personality, they generally tend to get along with other dogs and pets (except for hamsters, guinea pigs and other rodent or rodent-like creatures, which they are likely to view as prey). This is especially true if they have been raised with other animals. However, you should expect that your Affenpinscher will want to monopolize all of your attention, pushing his way in if you are playing with or petting one of your other pets. Because your Affenpinscher might attack a strange dog that he perceives as a threat, even one much larger than he is, it is important to keep him on his leash in public places. Keeping him on leash is also important for preventing him from running off after something that incites his interest, possibly into danger.

The same characteristics that make the Affenpinscher such a

At three years of age, this fun-loving Affenpinscher is Ch. Kyleakin Maid At Yarrow.

good watchdog mean that he generally is not a suitable breed for people with small children, although there are exceptions to this rule. Affens tend to guard their food and toys and may nip a child who attempts to take something they see as their property or who pesters them when they are sleeping or otherwise occupied. It is best if youngsters outside the family be told not to pet your Affen-pinscher, as he might feel threatened and snap at them. Although generally he will not bite hard enough to break the skin, he definitely will set limits on how much he allows himself to be handled. Children should also be discouraged from picking up your dog, as he might be injured if accidentally dropped. Additionally, a small child who is flailing his arms and legs about, screaming or running away might be perceived as prey by this breed, and an Affen will certainly go after what he thinks is prey.

Because of his small size, the Affenpinscher is well suited to indoor life, even in a small apartment. The Affenpinscher thrives on the company of his human companions and tends to stay close to his owners, whether indoors or outside on a country walk (though he must be on leash for safety). This is not a dog meant to be left in the yard for hours on end or in a kennel. In fact, because he is such a great climber, he is likely to attempt to escape from any such confinement. If you use a pen or metal

This lovely black female Affenpinscher is named Justyne (formally Ch. Hilane's Just Look At Me), pictured here with handler Kim Wedling. Justyne lives in Canada with her owner, Sandra Lex.

crate during house-training or to confine your dog when you are away, be certain that the pen or crate has a tight-fitting lid. We once knew a dog that hanged himself by pushing his head through a loose corner at the top of a pen and then was unable to get back down or out.

Affenpinschers living indoors, as they should, do not become acclimated to winter temperatures. Therefore, when walking your Affenpinscher outdoors in cold weather, be sure to provide him with a warm jacket. Quality pet-supply shops will have a variety of "winter-wear" for your stylish Affenpinscher.

THE IRRESISTIBLE AFFEN
People who own and love the Affenpinscher can't understand why, over the years, it has not become more popular. The following is a quotation taken from a "love letter" written by a new owner of an Affen puppy back to the breeder.

"We are totally, absolutely, hopelessly, all encompassingly in love with our little Meer-schaum! From the first second we laid eyes on his little black shoe-button eyes with matching nose and all those funny, fluffy feathers sticking haphazardly from his face—his dear charming, lovely face—we were hopelessly in love. I have had puppies (who ultimately became dogs, of course) all my life but this charm bracelet is so good, it's hard to believe he's only four and a half months old!"

There are many anecdotes that reflect the character and temperament of this breed. One that comes to mind is the story of a woman who had just returned with her husband from a trip abroad. The next day she had become ill and was at home recuperating on the sofa while her husband was at work. Suddenly loud, angry barking coming from the next room awakened her. The two sleeping Labrador Retrievers barely stirred while the barks and growls of growing intensity from her young Affenpinscher forced her to investigate. As she entered the next room she saw an intruder who had climbed part way through the open window but was being held at bay by her little dog whose hackles were up and who was poised ready to attack. When she and the intruder's eyes met, both abruptly turned, one towards the telephone, the other towards escape. Thank God for her little dog with his fearless determination! Obviously the intruder had been watching the house and assumed the inhabitants were still away. This woman believes that her little Affenpinscher probably saved her life.

One of the mottoes associated with this breed is "Affenpinschers —I'll bet you can't own just one!" Because they are so cute and small, new owners often want a playmate for their first dog. The introduction of a new puppy can cause the original dog some confusion and jealousy that may result in a lapse in his training. Dogs are territorial and scent marking is in their nature. Humans must be vigilant and persistent to keep a clean and odor-free home.

CARE AND TRAINING

The breed as a whole is unaware of its diminutive size and is willing and eager to take on any foe. This can and has resulted in some horrible occurrences. However, this same self-confident ego also makes for its endearing and comical quality. Obviously, this breed needs to be kept under control—on a leash, fenced in the yard or in an exercise pen for its own safety.

Because of its diminutive size and trainability, the Affenpinscher makes a good apartment dweller, though strict and consistent training is essential to make sure the Affenpinscher is an acceptable house pet. Of course, housebreaking is a necessity, and this requires patience, determination and consistency. There are reports of apartment dogs that have learned to use a cat litter box. The breed is very clever and can often outsmart its owners with all kinds of cute diversions.

In training your Affenpinscher, remember that he considers himself your partner, not a subject to be dominated, and tends to be quite independent-minded. Traditional dominance-based training methods generally do not work well with this breed. Praise, food and play are much more effective training tools than harsh corrections, which are likely to make your Affen stubbornly refuse to do what you want or even actively rebel. Newer gentler training methods that make the dog feel that "training is play" are extremely effective.

When training, do keep in mind that the Affenpinscher is very intelligent and becomes bored with constant repetition. Therefore, it is important to vary your training methods to keep your dog's attention. Of course, it can be very frustrating to try to train a dog that may dig in his heels or decide to give a comic performance (such as inappropriately flipping over on his back and waving his paws in the air) for a laughing audience. Nevertheless, owners have enjoyed great success with their Affenpinschers in the obedience ring. Even if you do not choose to compete at shows, obedience classes are a wonderful way to create a well-behaved companion, socialize your dog and strengthen the bond between you and your Affenpinscher.

HEALTH CONCERNS FOR THE AFFENPINSCHER BREED

In general, Affenpinschers are healthy dogs who lead active lifestyles for most of their lives. Your dog's coat will begin to turn gray around the face when he is only about five years old, with the gray spreading gradually until your pet looks like a senior by the time he is about ten. In general, Affenpinschers usually are considered seniors at about 8 years old and live to the age of 10 to 15 years.

When selecting a puppy, choose one that is active, clean and in good weight, with bright eyes and a shiny coat. Then take the pup to a veterinarian for a thorough examination upon bringing him home from the breeder. Like any other breed, your adult Affenpinscher should visit a veterinarian annually for a check-up and inoculations. As a senior, your pet may require a special diet or care, including more frequent routine visits to the vet. In addition to general health matters that apply to any breed, there are a few health issues that are more breed specific.

First, the way that an Affenpinscher's facial furnishings

grow around his large eyes makes it important that you keep his face clean and remove hairs in the corners of his eyes that may rub on the eyes themselves and cause injury. In rare cases, there may be hairs growing inside the eyelid that will irritate the eye and cause ulceration. In such a situation, these hairs should be regularly checked and professionally removed by a veterinary ophthalmologist. The eyebrows should be trimmed with scissors so that they do not obscure your dog's vision, and matter that collects in the inside corners of the eyes should be removed daily with a piece of cotton ball soaked in warm water.

One of the most serious problems in Affenpinschers is keratoconjunctivitis sicca, or "dry eye." It is not uncommon in this breed, particularly in older dogs. Because your dog cannot tell you that he is experiencing the mild discomfort that accompanies the disease in its early stages, it is up to you to be observant. If one of his eyes looks dull, rather than moist and shiny; if the eyes are red, accumulate excess mucus or are frequently encrusted with matter; or if you notice your dog's squinting or pawing at one or both eyes, take him to your vet.

Ask your veterinarian to perform a test to see if your dog is generating an adequate amount of tears. This will ensure that dry

eye, if present, is properly diagnosed. If untreated, an affected Affenpinscher will be prone to eye ulcers and eye infections that can lead to serious injury and even blindness. Treatment for dry eye generally consists of administering eye drops or ointment containing cyclosporine to your dog daily throughout his life. Cyclosporine has been shown to increase tear production in some cases, making treatment easier for the owner. In severe cases, surgery may be required to re-route a salivary gland to the eye, where it will provide a substitute source of moisture.

For Affenpinschers with uncropped drop ears, air circulation inside the ear may be impeded. In such a case, it is important to keep the insides of the ears clean and dry. Excess

Am. and Can. Ch. Dress Circle Grrilla and Ch. Hilane Dress Circle Ma Belle with the baby Ch. Hilane's Nyteflyte Flintyme. Owners, Marvin and Connie Clapp.

hair inside the ear canal can be removed with your thumb and finger. If you notice a discharge or foul odor from your dog's ear, he may have acquired an infection or ear mites and will require a specific diagnosis and medication from your vet. Untreated ear infections can lead to deafness, so this is not something to be neglected.

An Affenpinscher, like many other toy breeds, may retain some deciduous (baby) teeth after the adult teeth have emerged. This is particularly true of the canine teeth. You can try to wiggle these retained teeth to loosen them, but if they do not come out, your veterinarian eventually may have to extract them. If your pet is being spayed or neutered, this is also a good time to take care of these teeth so that the dog will not have to undergo additional anesthesia.

Affenpinschers, and many other toy breeds, are prone to patellar luxation (slipped knee caps) and other joint problems such as hip and elbow dysplasia. While, in general, Affens are light enough in weight that such problems do not become severely crippling, as they do in larger breeds, this is a matter for concern. Legg-Calve-Perthes disease is a genetic disorder of the hip joint that affects mainly small breeds and usually becomes evident before one year of age. Check with the breeder of your prospective puppy to be sure that the pup's parents have been tested for such problems, as many are hereditary in nature and affected dogs should not be bred. If you are considering doing advanced obedience or agility work with your dog, which involves jumping, be sure to have the dog tested first, as the stress of jumping could aggravate any joint problems.

ADVICE FOR NEW BREEDERS
For those who are thinking of breeding the Affenpinscher, there are a number of good books available that should be read before whelping a first litter. Be aware that, as with all toy dogs, the

Affenpinscher puppies, when acquired from well-respected breeders, will be sound, friendly and always ready for a little fun. This duo was bred by Nancy Baybutt.

litters are generally quite small, ranging from one to six puppies. The average litter size is between two and three. A few days before the due date have an x-ray taken of the female by your veterinarian. This will tell you the number and size of the puppies. C-sections are not common but could be required. All of this is expensive; therefore, this is not a moneymaking activity.

Be prepared. At birth the puppies usually weigh from 2 to 6 ounces. The puppies need to be whelped in a quiet, warm and clean environment and be carefully supervised. The mother needs to be watched carefully during and after whelping. She needs quiet support. With a first litter she may not know how to free the puppy from the sac and clean it. Have towels, washcloths, paper towels, sharp scissors, dental floss, a hemostat, plastic bags, cotton balls and a good book on breeding ready next to the whelping box. If this is the breeder's first litter, an experienced friend is a good thing to have.

The observers need to be aware of how and when problems can occur. Because of their size, a female may have difficulty delivering the first or the last puppy. Have a veterinarian "on call" to assist. Don't wait too long. Whelping a litter of toy puppies is a highly stressful activity.

Experience is a great teacher. Make sure the puppies nurse and that the mother has milk. She also must clean each puppy's vents to promote peristalsis. If the tails are going to be docked, this usually occurs when the healthy nursing puppies are two or three days old.

Special care should be given to the litter of puppies from four through seven weeks of age to make sure each puppy is socialized. This means that each puppy should be handled and exposed to new sights and sounds. This can include carrying them or allowing them to explore safely around the house, near the television or radio. Take them into the kitchen to familiarize them with those smells and sights, as well as the sounds of pots and pans. When friends come over, be sure they are allowed to play with each puppy. Early socialization is very important to minimize stranger and environmental fears.

No Affenpinscher puppy should leave his original home before 10 to 12 weeks of age. If the puppies are to have their ears cropped, this usually happens when they reach 3 pounds or 12 weeks. The reason for this older age is because the trauma of the surgery and the effects of the anesthesia are less dangerous. There have been reports of the too-small or too-young puppy dying during or after the ear cropping.

BREED STANDARD FOR THE

AFFENPINSCHER

Each breed recognized by the American Kennel Club (AKC) has an approved breed standard, a word picture of how the ideal breed representative appears. From time to time, the parent club elects to alter the breed standard for the sake of clarity or a slight change in focus. The third and latest version was approved July 27, 2000. This is a revision of the standard that was approved on May 31, 1990. The first AKC standard dates back to September 15, 1936, when the Affenpinscher was first recognized.

The italicized analyses assist the reader in interpreting the current Affenpinscher standard. Whether you are a newcomer to the breed or an experienced show judge, you will find all the important terminology and concepts explained here to assist you in better understanding what the standard intends to say.

THE AKC STANDARD FOR THE AFFENPINSCHER

General Appearance: The Affenpinscher is a balanced, wiry-haired terrier-like toy dog whose intelligence and demeanor make it a good house pet. Originating in Germany, the name Affenpinscher means "monkey-like terrier." The breed was developed to rid the kitchens, granaries and stables of rodents. In France the breed is described as the "Diablotin Moustachu" or the "moustached little devil." Both describe the appearance and attitude of this delightful breed. The total overall appearance of the

---

READING THE BREED STANDARD
What does the breed standard mean to you, the owner or prospective owner of a pet Affenpinscher? "Pet-quality" Affenpinschers still make delightful pets, but they should be spayed or neutered to avoid perpetuating their faults. Do not be offended when a responsible breeder insists that you neuter your pet; this shows that he has the long-term welfare of the breed at heart. While many deviations from the breed standard may be obvious only to a knowledgeable fancier, you should be familiar enough with the breed standard to ensure that your puppy will look and behave like a typical representative of this wonderful breed you have chosen, even if you have no aspirations to show.

Affenpinscher is more important than any individual characteristic. He is described as having a neat, but shaggy, appearance.

The first concept to be discussed is that of balance. According to the dictionary, "balance" means "harmonious proportions." The Affenpinscher is a proportionate little dog in a shaggy package. The wiry hair or hard shaggy coat and the stand-off face and head hair are very important to the look of this breed. The Affenpinscher should not be overly stripped, sculpted or sprayed up. It should however look like a show dog, shaped and neatened.

Next, "terrier-like toy dog" refers to the general look of a small but sturdy, not delicate, rather spunky, self-assured, strong-willed, inquisitive and mischievous little dog. The appropriate attitude is most evident when the dog is comfortable and secure in his surroundings.

When evaluating the Affenpinscher, it is important to look at the overall impression. Not any one aspect or feature is of more value or of more importance than any other. Keep in mind the original function of this breed was to catch rodents. Therefore, it must be alert, quick, flexible and aggressive toward things that appear to be prey.

Size, Proportion, Substance: A sturdy, compact little dog of medium bone, not delicate in any way. Preferred height at the withers

Illustration of adult dog showing correct balance, structure and type.

is between 9.5 and 11.5 inches. Withers height is approximately the same as the length of the body from the point of the shoulder to the point of the buttocks, giving a square appearance. The female may be slightly longer.

The purpose of describing the substance of the Affenpinscher as a "sturdy, compact little dog of medium bone" is to maintain a sound toy dog that does not become so fine or weak as not to be able to satisfy its function. At the same time the breed should not become too coarse and too large. It is true that the precursor of the breed at the beginning of the 20th century was bigger and coarser and that the Miniature Schnauzer and the Affenpinscher-type dog came from the same litter. Today breeders will occasionally produce a

Head study showing correct structure and type.

"throwback," a puppy who will become 14 to 16 inches tall. This specimen is not a "toy" in size or quality.

This revised standard allows for a 2-inch spread in the height at the withers. This reflects the moderation of size, which has been consistent in the breed over the past 20 years. The old standard stated "should not exceed 10.25 inches in any case." The second stated "with 10.25 inches being the ideal." In the author's opinion, the removal of this size suggestion can be a problem for the breed. It is hoped that this spread in the desirable height will keep the emphasis on soundness, type and overall quality of the dog rather than on size, but the larger should not be considered better. The square-appearing dog is most typical of the breed. In reality, most are half an inch longer than they are tall.

Head: The head is in proportion to the body, carried confidently with monkey-like facial expression. Eyes—Round, dark, brilliant, and of medium size in proportion to the head but not bulging or protruding. Eye rims are black. Ears—Cropped to a point, set high and standing erect; or natural, standing erect, semi-erect or dropped. All of the above types of ears if symmetrical are acceptable as long as the monkey-like expression is maintained. Skull—Round and domed but not coarse. Stop—Well-defined. Muzzle—Short and narrowing slightly to a blunt nose. The length of the muzzle is approximately the same as the distance between the eyes. Nose—Black, turned neither up nor down. Lips—Black, with prominent lower lip. Bite—Slightly undershot. A level bite is acceptable if the monkey-like expression is maintained. An overshot bite is to be severely penalized. A wry mouth is a serious fault. The teeth and tongue do not show when the mouth is closed. The lower jaw is broad enough for the lower teeth to be straight and even.

Three times the phrase "monkey-like expression" is reiterated in the above section concerning the head. When adding up the descriptions of the round dark eye, the round domed skull, the short level muzzle and the prominent lips, the image of a monkey-like creature does come to mind. Since most monkeys do not have stand-off hair on their faces, the personality and the whimsical antics of the Affenpinscher must support the impression. No other breed combines the physical features with the intent stare, the tilting head and the comic agility, which can so clearly remind one of another species.

The kind of ears is not an issue. Cropped or natural as long as both ears are symmetrical; then they are not a concern.

Four very important elements of the Affenpinscher's head help to distinguish it from other toy breeds. First, the eyes, though full, are not as large or as protruding as those of the Brussels Griffon. Second, the muzzle is as long as the distance of the space between the inside corners of the eyes. Third, the nose neither turns up as in the brachycephalic head type of the Pekingese, Pug or the Brussels Griffon nor does it turn down creating a down-faced, unpleasing expression. Fourth, the slightly protruding lower lip gives a pouty look to the face, which adds to this distinctive expression.

Neck, Topline and Body: Neck—Short and straight. Topline—Straight and level. Body—The chest is moderately broad and deep; ribs are moderately sprung. Tuck up is slight. The back is short and level with a strong loin. The croup has just a perceptible curve. The tail may be docked or natural. A docked tail is generally between 1- and 2-inches long; set high and carried erect. The natural tail is set high and carried gently up over the back while moving. The type of tail is not a major consideration.

The neck is described as "short and straight": "short" as opposed to long or reachy; "straight" meaning without much curve on either the topline or underside of the throat. Much of this image can be controlled by the amount of hair that is left in this area and how it is groomed. If the neck is too short, then the dog can look "stuffy" or out of proportion.

The shape of the body can be described as an oval that is wider at the top, rather egg-shaped but broader. The ribs taper inward slightly toward the bottom. The depth of the chest reaches just to the elbow. In the mature dog the ratio of the depth of chest to the length of leg is about 1 to 1. This image is sometimes distorted by the length and density of the furnishings on the underline. These furnishings also add to the image that there is not much tuck up in the underline.

One of the most obvious changes from the oldest standard is the acceptance of the natural ears and tail. Only the "natural" Affenpinscher can be shown in England and most of Europe and is seen more and more in North America. It is a different look but with the proper grooming the breed doesn't lose its typical expression. Possibly the natural curved tail may even add to the monkey-like appearance.

With the younger dogs the natural tail may stand almost straight in the air. As he or she matures it will curve over the back. When standing relaxed the tail may drop down.

Forequarters: The front angulation is moderate. Shoulders—With moderate layback. The lengths of the shoulder blade and upper arm are about equal. Elbows—Close to the body. Front Legs—Straight when viewed from any direction. Pasterns—Short and straight. Dewclaws—Generally removed. Feet—Small, round and compact with black pads and nails.

When looking at all of the angles of the joints in the fore-quarters, "moderate" should be the word that comes to mind; 25 to 40 degrees of layback at the shoulder is appropriate for this breed. The front angulation should match the rear angulation.

The sentence that causes some concern is, "The lengths of the shoulder blade and upper arm are about equal." In the previous standard, "the lengths of the upper arm and the lower arm" were about equal. The purpose for comparing the upper and lower arm was to maintain the breed's characteristic jaunty movement. The Affenpinscher does not have the "lift" or "hackney" gait of the Italian Greyhound or the Miniature Pinscher. Both of these breeds have a longer lower arm.

Hindquarters: The rear angulation is moderate to match the front. Hindlegs—Straight when viewed from behind. From the side, hindlegs are set under the body to maintain a square appearance. The lengths of the upper thigh and the second thigh are about equal with moderate bend to stifle. Hock—Moderately angulated.

It is important to remember that "angulation" refers to all of the joints, the places where the bones or corresponding structures are joined, in the rear area. In the old standard, the statement "without much bend at hock" was often misinterpreted to mean that the Affenpinscher should have straight rear angulation. When reading the first standard, the reference is to the front legs, which "should be as straight as possible." The view is meant to be from the front. So it follows that the phrase "without

COLOR POSSIBILITIES

The AKC standard does not have the same color restrictions as the standards of some other countries. It allows Affenpinschers in the show ring to be black, gray, silver, symmetrically marked black and tan, red (varying from brownish red to orangey tan) or belge (a color similar to agouti, with alternating bands of color on each hair). Color is never a consideration in the US unlike in Europe, where black and black and tan are the only acceptable colors for the breed.

much bend at hock" was intended to mean when viewed from the rear, thus trying to avoid cow hocks or bow hocks.

For a correctly set up moderately angulated rear, if a plumb line were dropped from the point of the buttocks it would fall along the posterior edge of the rear pastern, thus maintaining the overall square appearance desired in this breed. This is the ideal but it is preferred to err on the side of more angulation, not less. Weak rears have been a problem for the Affenpinscher.

Coat: Dense hair, rough, harsh, about 1 inch in length on the shoulders and body. It may be shorter on the rear and tail. Head, neck, chest, stomach and legs have longer, less harsh coat. The mature Affenpinscher has a mane or cape of strong hair that blends into the back coat at the withers area. The longer hair on the head, eyebrows and beard stands off and frames the face to emphasize the monkey-like expression. Hair on the ears is cut very short. A correct coat needs little grooming to blend the various lengths of hair to maintain a neat but shaggy appearance.

Everyone seems to have an opinion on what kind of coat and how much grooming are correct. The controversy continues, but a happy medium is gradually emerging. Some professional handlers have tended to over-groom, taking

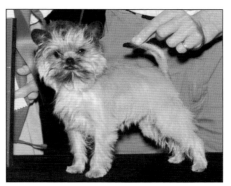

Quality should be recognizable from puppyhood, as displayed by the author's Best in Match-winning redhead, Ch. Hilane's I Love Lucy.

the "jacket" down to about half an inch in length and pulling out most of the furnishings on the legs. Even though this extreme look is successful in the show ring, it does not make it correct. Historically the Affenpinscher has had a scruffier look than terriers or the Brussels Griffon. The 1-inch length of hair on the body gives the breed its shaggy characteristic look. A question has been raised concerning the mane or cape on the neck and shoulders. The word "cape" seems more appropriate. A "mane" suggests a ruff that sticks out and would overload the front and destroy the balance.

Here's Ch. Tamarin Talullah, bred by Beth K. Sweigart, Letisha Wubbel and owner Doris Tolone.

FAULTS IN THE AFFENPINSCHER

Too narrow and pinched front and rear; toes out in front; straight in rear.

Roached back; low tail set; weak pasterns; flat feet.

Long back and coat excessively long, which usually means that it lacks the correct wiry texture.

Low on leg; front too wide with heavy shoulders; weak rear.

Color: Black, gray, silver, red or black and tan, or belge are all acceptable. Blacks may have a rusty cast or a few white or silver hairs mixed with the black. Reds may vary from brownish red to an orangey tan. Belge has black, brown and/or white hairs mixed with the red. With the various colors, the furnishings may be a bit lighter. Some dogs have black masks. A small white spot on the chest is not penalized, but large white patches are undesirable. Color is not a major consideration.

In continental Europe and England black and black and tan are the only acceptable colors. The old standard stated that "the best color is black." A careful look at the history of the breed reveals that until 1937 many colors existed and, in fact, the majority were the colors other than black. Today we question the reasons for limiting the colors. When considering the very small gene pool, it seems counterproductive to restrict the acceptance of other colors. In the mid-1960s several breeders worked hard to bring back many of the original colors. These colors flourish today and are credited with improving the coat texture and the rich black color, which is still respected. Bearing all this in mind, color, nevertheless, should never be a determining factor in judging the Affenpinscher.

Gait: Light, free, sound, balanced, confident, the Affenpinscher carries itself with comic seriousness. Viewed from the front or rear while walking, the legs move parallel to each other. Trotting, the feet will converge toward a midline as speed increases. Unsound gait is to be heavily penalized.

More could be said that would distinguish the Affenpinscher's movement. One word that might be used is "jaunty," defined as "easy and careless; gay and swaggering; sprightly; perky." Another word that comes from Germany, which describes the gait, is trippeln, *meaning small, carefully placed or precise steps. Both of these help to define the characteristic gait.*

The exaggerated reach and drive appropriate for many other breeds is incorrect for the Affenpinscher. This breed requires agility and spring in its movement to enable it to catch small rodents. The Affenpinscher didn't need to race long distances or cover a lot of ground but instead to lie in wait and pounce on his prey. Thus the correct gait is light and springy. In the show ring the Affenpinscher should be moved at a speed which best shows off this characteristic gait and not raced around the ring.

The immature Affenpinscher can have quite a different gait and look. As this breed fills out, or "bodies up," rather remarkable changes occur. Often the young

dog will achieve his length of leg and body but the chest does not "drop" or the ribs "spring." This lack of substance affects the movement as well as the overall appearance of the youngster. Since many breeders show these young dogs, some judges and spectators find it difficult to distinguish the correct appearance and gait for the breed. Generally the breed matures between two and three years of age.

Temperament: General demeanor is game, alert and inquisitive with great loyalty and affection toward its master and friends. The breed is generally quiet but can become vehemently excited when threatened or attacked and is fearless toward any aggressor.

The comfortable and confident Affenpinscher reflects the above characteristics. But this breed can demonstrate a strong will if a seeming threat occurs. Sometimes a stranger or a frightening sound can cause an Affenpinscher to hysterically retreat or seek shelter. Patience usually brings such a dog around. The breed's expression reveals a "thinking" dog. The Affenpinscher owner needs to be consistent and definite in the expectations for the dog. This breed is remarkably intelligent and can be quite manipulative. Gentle and loving discipline is important for co-existence with this breed.

AFFENPINSCHER

SELECTING AN AFFENPINSCHER BREEDER AND PUPPY

The Affenpinscher is a sturdy, intelligent, terrier-like toy dog that is generally well suited to life in today's smaller living quarters. Early socialization of this breed is critical, so be sure you buy from a responsible breeder who has given the puppies lots of loving attention and exposed them to a wide variety of people, sights, sounds and smells. Because toy puppies are so tiny and fragile, it is unlikely that you will be allowed to take your puppy home until he is 12 weeks old. Affenpinschers are relatively rare and have small litters, as few as two to three puppies, so do not be surprised if you must wait quite some time to obtain a puppy from a reputable breeder of quality dogs.

Trusted places to begin your search are the American Kennel Club (www.akc.org) and the Affenpinscher Club of America (www.affenpinscher.org), the AKC-recognized national club for the breed. The Affenpinscher Club of America (ACA) offers a wealth of information on the breed for newcomers and experienced fanciers alike. They also offer a breeder referral service, through which you can locate ACA member breeders in your part of the country. ACA breeders must abide by a code of ethics in their breeding programs; this offers assurance to the prospective Affen owner, who is searching for a reputable breeder whom he can trust. If you are interested in an adult Affen rather than a puppy, the ACA also has an active rescue program that can help you find an Affenpinscher in need of a new home.

When you are trying to decide which puppy is right for you,

When purchasing an Affenpinscher from an established kennel, you will get a healthy, happy puppy at a fair price. Your homework will pay off, so choose with your head and not your heart. Breeder, Nancy Baybutt.

THE FAMILY TREE

Your puppy's pedigree is his family tree. Just as a child may resemble his parents and grandparents, so too will a puppy reflect the qualities, good and bad, of his ancestors, especially those in the first two generations. Therefore it's important to know as much as possible about a puppy's immediate relatives. Reputable and experienced breeders should be able to explain the pedigree and why they chose to breed from the particular dogs they used.

problems related to temperament and health that have been encountered with poorly bred puppies are, indeed, tragic.

A responsible breeder will likely ask you a lot of questions to be sure that you will provide a suitable home for an Affenpinscher puppy. Do not be offended, as these questions will also help ensure that you get the puppy that best suits your personality and lifestyle. Do be forewarned that if you have small children, the Affenpinscher is probably not an appropriate breed for you. Before you begin your puppy search, you should read as

study the breed standard and ask to see at least the dam, all of the puppies in the litter and other relatives if possible. If you are lucky, the sire will be on the premises, though this is not always the case.

If you are planning on buying an Affenpinscher, try to visit the prospective pet in his original environment. Seeing the temperament of the parents and the puppy in his own home will help to identify personality traits. If this is impossible, then it's important to make contact with other Affen owners and the breed club to find out about the reputation of the breeder of your prospective puppy. Horror stories abound from people who have impulsively purchased a cute little puppy and have paid more money than the cost of a show potential from a reputable breeder. The

It's not easy to resist the allure of an Affenpinscher baby. Never be seduced by cuteness alone. This alluring darling is "Tina," Periwinkle Private Dancer at a tender nine weeks of age.

much as you can about the breed and rank the qualities that are most important to you. Be sure to make your wishes clear to the breeder, who has been observing the puppies since birth and will be more familiar with their individual characteristics than you could be during a brief visit. Also, if you aspire to show your Affen, the breeder can use his experience to predict as best he can which pup shows the most promise.

When you go to visit the breeder and litter, you should have already decided whether you want a dog that is more calm and quiet or more outgoing and assertive. Observe each puppy carefully. All puppies are cute, of course, but which one seems to be the most curious, the most playful, etc? Which might make the best watchdog or the sturdiest companion if you want the dog to

At this breeder's home, the adult dogs other than the dam are kept in a different area than the tiny puppies.

accompany you on long walks?

It is not at all uncommon for Affenpinschers to be a bit wary of strangers at first, but the puppies should soon come to you in familiar surroundings with a bit of encouragement from their breeder. An occasional puppy may be quite standoffish, which may indicate more caution than you desire. The ideal puppy for the show or obedience ring is extremely outgoing. While Affenpinschers are often stubborn, try holding a puppy in your arms on his back

for a moment. If the pup struggles frantically to get away rather than relaxing in your arms, he may become a very dominant dog that might be more difficult to train.

Ask which health tests have been performed on the puppy and the parents, ask to see documentation of the test results and ask what sort of written health guarantee the breeder will provide. At the very least, you should be given a few days to take the puppy to your veterinarian for a thorough check-up and be able to return the pup for a full refund if any problems are found. It is not enough to be able to exchange one sickly puppy for another from the same inferior litter!

Older Affenpinschers, retired show dogs or retired breeding animals that have been spayed or neutered, often make excellent pets. This breed is highly trainable and very adaptable if introduced into the family in a quiet and consistent way. Most older dogs accept crate training and appreciate the scheduled quiet time in a comfortable enclosure. Be sure to allow the dog to visit his toilet area immediately after the rest. Gradually introduce the newly adopted adult into a new or different environment after it has been let out and exercised for an adequate length of time. A secure exercise pen or a fenced-in yard is necessary for all small dogs.

A COMMITTED NEW OWNER

By now you should understand what makes the Affenpinscher a most unique and special dog, one that you feel may fit nicely into your family and lifestyle. If you have researched breeders, you should be able to recognize a knowledgeable and responsible Affenpinscher breeder who cares

SELECTING FROM THE LITTER

Before you visit a litter of puppies, promise yourself that you won't fall for the first pretty face you see! Decide on your goals for your puppy—show prospect, obedience competitor, family companion—and then look for a puppy who displays the appropriate qualities. In most litters, there is an alpha pup (the bossy puppy), and occasionally a shy fellow who is less confident, with the rest of the litter falling somewhere in the middle. "Middle-of-the-roaders" are safe bets for most families and novices.

not only about his pups but also about what kind of owner you will be. If you have completed the final step in your new journey, you have found a litter, or possibly two, of quality Affenpinscher pups.

A visit with the puppies and their breeder should be an education in itself. Breed research, breeder selection and puppy visitation are very important aspects of finding the puppy of your dreams. Beyond that, these things also lay the foundation for a successful future with your pup. As we've mentioned, puppy personalities within each litter vary, from the shy and easygoing puppy to the one who is dominant and assertive, with most pups falling somewhere in between. By spending time with the puppies you will be able to recognize certain behaviors and what these behaviors indicate about each pup's temperament. Which type of pup will complement your family dynamics is best

NO AFFEN BEFORE HIS TIME
Breeders of most breeds of dog release puppies when they are eight to ten weeks of age. Toy breeds like the Affenpinscher are not released until around 12 weeks, given their petite sizes. If a breeder has a puppy that is 16 weeks of age or older, the puppy should be well socialized and well on his way to being house-trained. Be sure that he is otherwise healthy before deciding to take him home.

determined by observing the puppies in action within their "pack" and seeing which one appeals to you most. Your breeder's expertise and recommendations are valuable. Although you may fall in love with a bold and brassy male, the breeder may suggest that another pup would be best for you. The breeder's experience in rearing Affenpinscher pups and matching their temperaments with appropriate humans offers the best assurance that your pup will meet your needs and expectations. The type of puppy that you select is just as important as your decision that the Affenpinscher is the breed for you.

Your Affenpinscher puppy is a living sentient being that will be dependent on you for basic survival for his entire life. Beyond the basics of survival—food, water, shelter and protection—he needs much, much more. The new

Breeders allow prospective owners to visit the litter before the pups are old enough for new homes. Take advantage of the opportunity, as you will learn so much from observing the pups, not to mention having a lot of fun while doing so.

pup needs love, nurturing and a proper canine education to mold him into a responsible, well-behaved canine citizen. Your Affenpinscher's health and good manners will need consistent monitoring and regular "tune-ups," so your job as a responsible

Puppies aren't always on the go; they spend much of their time resting and napping. At six weeks of age, this pup is not yet ready to leave the breeder.

PEDIGREE VS. REGISTRATION CERTIFICATE

Too often new owners are confused between these two important documents. Your puppy's pedigree, essentially a family tree, is a written record of a dog's genealogy of three generations or more. The pedigree will show you the names as well as performance titles of all dogs in your pup's background. Your breeder must provide you with a registration application, with his part properly filled out. You must complete the application and send it to the AKC with the proper fee. Every puppy must come from a litter that has been AKC-registered by the breeder, born in the US and from a sire and dam that are also registered with the AKC.

The seller must provide you with complete records to identify the puppy. The AKC requires that the seller provide the buyer with the following: breed; sex, color and markings; date of birth; litter number (when available); names and registration numbers of the parents; breeder's name; and date sold or delivered.

dog owner will be ongoing throughout every stage of his life. If you are not prepared to accept these responsibilities and commit to them for upwards of the next decade, then you are not prepared to own a dog of any breed.

Remember that owning an Affenpinscher is a serious commitment that should not be undertaken lightly. A dog is a living thing that is not disposable. If you have any doubts about whether this is the right breed for you, or if you are not willing to provide a caring home for your pet for his entire lifetime, do not buy the dog. Remember, the Affenpinscher can live to be 15 years of age, so this is no short-term commitment. Nevertheless, unforeseen circumstances do occur. It is therefore appropriate to ask what the breeder would do if for some extraordinary reason you were unable to provide a home for your Affenpinscher in the future. Most responsible breeders will be willing to help you find a loving home for a dog they have bred, but this does not mean that you should back out of

A shallow water bowl or even a plate is a good feeding vessel for the short-faced Affenpinscher.

warmth and familiarity of his mom and littermates to the brand-new environment of his new home and human family. You will be too busy to stock up and prepare your house after your pup comes home, that's for sure. Imagine how a pup must feel upon being transported to a strange new place. It's up to you to comfort him and to let your little pup know that he is going to be happy with you.

FOOD AND WATER BOWLS

Your puppy will need separate bowls for his food and water. Stainless steel pans are generally preferred over plastic bowls since they sterilize better and pups are less inclined to chew on the metal. Heavy-duty ceramic bowls are popular as well. Shallow bowls are best for the short-

your commitment to your dog except in the most extenuating circumstances.

Although the responsibilities of owning a dog may at times tax your patience, the joy of living with your Affenpinscher far outweighs the workload, and a well-mannered adult dog is worth your time and effort. Before your very eyes, your new charge will grow up to be your most loyal friend, amusing you and devoted to you unconditionally.

YOUR AFFENPINSCHER SHOPPING LIST

Just as expectant parents prepare a nursery for their baby, so should you ready your home for the arrival of your Affenpinscher pup. If you have the necessary puppy supplies purchased and in place before he comes home, it will ease the puppy's transition from the

GETTING ACQUAINTED

When visiting a litter, ask the breeder for suggestions on how best to interact with the puppies. If possible, get right into the middle of the pack and sit down with them. Observe which pups climb into your lap and which ones shy away. Toss a toy for them to chase and bring back to you. It's easy to fall in love with the puppy who picks you, but keep your lifestyle, family and future objectives in mind before you make your final decision.

muzzled Affenpinscher. Buy bowls in a size that will suit your Affen as both pup and adult.

THE DOG CRATE

If you think that crates are tools of punishment and confinement for when a dog has misbehaved, think again. Most breeders and almost all trainers recommend a crate as the preferred house-training aid as well as for all-around puppy training and safety. Because dogs are natural den creatures that prefer cave-like environments, the benefits of crate use are many. The crate provides the puppy with his very own "safe house," a cozy place to sleep, take a break or seek comfort with a favorite toy; a travel aid to house your dog when on the road, at motels or at the vet's office; a training aid to help teach your puppy proper toileting habits; and

a place of solitude when non-dog people happen to drop by and don't want a lively puppy—or even a well-behaved adult dog—saying hello or begging for their attention.

Crates come in several types, although the wire crate and the fiberglass airline-type crate are the most popular. Both are safe and your puppy will adjust to either one, so the choice is up to you. The wire crates offer better visibility for the pup as well as better ventilation. Many of the wire crates easily fold into suitcase-size carriers. The fiberglass crates, similar to those used by the airlines for animal transport, are sturdier and more den-like. However, the fiberglass crates do not fold down and are less ventilated than wire crates, which can be problematic in hot weather. Some of the newer crates are made of heavy plastic mesh; they are very lightweight and fold up into slim-line suitcases. However, a mesh crate might not

The three most common crate types: mesh on the left, wire on the right and fiberglass on top. The Affenpinscher is a toy dog, so it will be easy to buy a crate that will comfortably house him as a pup and as an adult.

COST OF OWNERSHIP
The purchase price of your puppy is merely the first expense in the typical dog budget. Quality dog food, veterinary care (sickness and health maintenance), dog supplies and grooming costs will add up to big bucks every year. Can you adequately afford to support a canine addition to the family?

TIDY BOY

Clean by nature, dogs do not like to soil their dens, which in effect are their crates or sleeping quarters. Unless not feeling well, dogs will not defecate or urinate in their crates. Crate training capitalizes on the dog's natural desire to keep his den clean. Be conscientious about giving the puppy as many opportunities to relieve himself outdoors as possible. Reward the puppy for correct behavior. Praise him and pat him whenever he "goes" in the correct location. Even the tidiest of puppies can have potty accidents, so be patient and dedicate more energy to helping your puppy achieve a clean lifestyle.

be suitable for a pup with manic chewing habits.

Don't bother with a puppy-sized crate. A small crate will suffice for both a puppy and fully grown Affenpinscher, provided the crate allows him enough room to lie down, stand up and turn around at his adult size.

BEDDING AND CRATE PADS

Your puppy will enjoy some type of soft bedding in his "room" (the crate), something he can snuggle into to feel cozy and secure. Old towels or blankets are good choices for a young pup, since he may (and probably will) have a toileting accident or two in the crate or decide to chew on the bedding material. Once he is fully trained and out of the early chewing stage, you can replace the puppy bedding with a permanent crate pad if you prefer. Crate pads and other dog beds run the gamut from inexpensive to high-end doggie-designer styles, but don't splurge on the good stuff until you are sure that your puppy is reliable and won't tear it up or make a mess on it.

PUPPY TOYS

Just as infants and older children require objects to stimulate their minds and bodies, puppies need toys to entertain their curious brains, wiggly paws and achy teeth. A fun array of safe doggie toys will help satisfy your puppy's chewing instincts and distract him from gnawing on the leg of your antique chair or your new leather sofa. Most puppy toys are cute and look as if they would be a lot of fun, but not all are necessarily safe or good for your puppy, so use caution when you go puppy-toy shopping.

Although Affens are not known to be voracious chewers like many other dogs, they still enjoy chewing. The best "chewcifiers" are nylon and hard rubber bones which are safe to gnaw on and come in sizes appropriate for all age groups and breeds. Affenpinschers also like hard dog biscuits. Be especially careful of natural bones, which can splinter or develop dangerous sharp edges; pups can easily swallow or choke on those bone splinters. Veterinarians often tell of surgical nightmares involving bits of splintered bone because in addition to the danger of choking, the sharp pieces can damage the intestinal tract if swallowed.

> **TEETHING TIME**
>
> All puppies chew. It's normal canine behavior. Chewing just plain feels good to a puppy, especially during the three- to five-month teething period when the adult teeth are breaking through the gums. Rather than attempting to eliminate such a strong natural chewing instinct, you will be more successful if you redirect it and teach your puppy what he may or may not chew. Correct inappropriate chewing with a sharp "No!" and offer him a chew toy, praising him when he takes it. Don't become discouraged. Chewing usually decreases after the adult teeth have come in.

Similarly, rawhide chews, while a favorite of most dogs and puppies, can be equally dangerous. Pieces of rawhide are easily swallowed after they get soft and gummy from chewing, and dogs have been known to choke on pieces of ingested rawhide. Rawhide chews should be offered only when you can supervise the puppy.

Soft woolly toys are favorites of many puppies. They come in a wide variety of cute shapes and sizes; some look like little stuffed animals. However, breeders advise owners to be cautious with stuffed toys, as they may incite your Affenpinscher's deep-rooted terrier instincts. As such, these toys can become de-stuffed in no time; likewise for squeaky toys. If destroyed, the pieces can be dangerous if swallowed.

Braided rope toys are similar in that they are fun to chew and toss around, but they shred easily and the strings are easy to swal-

Irresistible, amusing and mischievous, the Affenpinscher puppy is all these and more. Breeder, Nancy Baybutt.

TOYS 'R SAFE

The vast array of tantalizing puppy toys is staggering. Stroll through any pet shop or pet-supply outlet and you will see that the choices can be overwhelming. However, not all dog toys are safe or sensible. Most very young puppies enjoy soft woolly toys that they can snuggle with and carry around. (You know they have outgrown them when they shred them up!) Avoid toys that have buttons, tabs or other enhancements that can be chewed off and swallowed. Soft toys that squeak are fun, but make sure your puppy does not disembowel the toy and remove (and swallow) the squeaker. Toys that rattle or make noise can excite a puppy, but they present the same danger as the squeaky kind and so require supervision. Hard rubber toys that bounce can also entertain a pup, but make sure that the toy is too big for your pup to swallow.

low. The strings are not digestible, and if the puppy doesn't pass them in his stool, he could end up at the vet's office. As with rawhides, your puppy should be closely monitored with rope toys.

If you believe that your pup has ingested one of these forbidden objects, check his stool for the next couple of days to see if he passes them when he defecates. At the same time, also watch for signs of intestinal distress. A call to your veterinarian might be in order to get his advice and to be on the safe side.

An all-time favorite toy for puppies (young and old!) is the empty gallon milk jug. Hard plastic juice containers—46 ounces or more—are also excellent. Such containers make lots of noise when they are batted about, and puppies go crazy with delight as they play with them. However, they don't often last very long, so be sure to remove and replace them when they get chewed up.

A word of caution about homemade toys: be careful with your choices of non-traditional play objects. Never use old shoes or socks, since a puppy cannot distinguish between the old ones on which he's allowed to chew and the new ones in your closet that are strictly off limits. That principle applies to anything that resembles something that you don't want your puppy to chew.

COLLARS

A lightweight nylon collar is the best choice for a very young pup. Quick-click collars are easy to put on and remove, and they can be adjusted as the puppy grows. Introduce him to his collar as soon as he comes home to get him accustomed to wearing it. He'll get used to it quickly and won't mind a bit. Make sure that it is snug enough that it won't slip off, yet loose enough to be comfortable for the pup. You should be able to slip two fingers between the collar and his neck. Check the collar often, as puppies grow in spurts, and his collar can become too tight almost overnight. Choke collars should never be used on an Affenpinscher puppy or adult. Choke collars are not recommended for use on small dogs; furthermore, a choke collar is too harsh of a training tool for this sensitive breed. You may want to consider a harness when walking your Affenpinscher, as some owners feel that they are more comfortable for small dogs than traditional collars.

LEASHES

A 6-foot nylon lead is an excellent choice for a young puppy. It is lightweight and not as tempting to chew as a leather lead. You can switch to a 6-foot leather lead if you choose after your pup has grown and is used to walking politely on a lead. For initial

Toys and a soft bed to cuddle up on—this young Affenpinscher has all he needs to keep busy and cozy.

puppy walks and house-training purposes, you should invest in a shorter lead so that you have more control over the puppy. At first, you don't want him wandering too far away from you, and when taking him out for toileting you will want to keep him in the specific area chosen for his potty spot.

Once the puppy is heel-trained with a traditional leash, you can consider purchasing a retractable lead. A retractable lead is excellent for walking adult dogs that are already leash-wise. This type of lead expands to allow the dog to roam farther away from you and explore a wider area when out walking and also retracts when you need to keep him close to you.

HOME SAFETY FOR YOUR PUPPY

The importance of puppy-proofing cannot be overstated. In addition to making your house comfortable for your Affenpinscher's arrival, you also must make sure that your house is safe for your puppy before you bring him home. There are countless hazards in the owner's personal living environment that a pup can sniff, chew, swallow or destroy. Many are obvious; others are not. Do a thorough advance house check to remove or rearrange those things that could hurt your puppy, keeping any potentially dangerous items out of areas to which he will have access.

Electrical cords are especially dangerous, since puppies view them as irresistible chew toys. Unplug and remove all exposed cords or fasten them beneath the baseboards where the puppy cannot reach them. Veterinarians and firefighters can tell you horror stories about electrical burns and house fires that resulted from puppy-chewed electrical cords. Consider this a most serious precaution for your puppy and the rest of your family.

Scout your home for tiny objects that the pup might find. Keep medication bottles and cleaning supplies well out of reach, and do the same with waste baskets and other trash containers. It goes without saying that you should not use rodent poison or other toxic chemicals in any puppy area and that you must keep such containers safely locked up. You will be amazed at how many places a curious puppy can discover!

Once your house has cleared inspection, check your yard. A sturdy fence, well embedded into the ground, will give your dog a safe place to play and potty. However, do not let a fence give you a false sense of security—the Affen not only looks like a monkey but also climbs like one! This ability, combined with his terrier digging talents, makes fencing a major consideration for owners. The best way to contain these escape artists is to embed the fence at least a foot deep into the ground and avoid chain-link type fencing that the dog can use as a "ladder" to climb out. Check the fence periodically for necessary repairs. If there is a weak area or a space to squeeze through, you can be sure that a determined Affenpinscher will discover it. If your dog spends any time in a dog run or pen, make sure that the enclosure has a secure covering.

The garage and shed can be hazardous places for a pup, as things like fertilizers, chemicals and tools are usually kept there. It's best to keep these areas off limits to the dog. Antifreeze is especially dangerous to dogs, as they find the taste appealing and it takes only a few licks from the driveway to kill a dog, puppy or adult, small breed or large.

VISITING THE VETERINARIAN
A good veterinarian is your Affenpinscher puppy's best health-insurance policy. If you do not already have a vet, ask friends and experienced dog people in your area for recommendations so that you can select a vet before you bring your Affenpinscher puppy home. Also arrange for your puppy's first veterinary examination beforehand, since many vets do not have appointments available immediately and your puppy should visit the vet within a day

A safe doggie door is one that allows your Affenpinscher, and only your Affenpinscher, access to go from the house to the fenced yard as he pleases.

or so of coming home.

It's important to make sure that your puppy's first visit to the vet is a pleasant and positive one. The vet should take great care to befriend the pup and handle him gently to make their first meeting a positive experience. The vet will give the pup a thorough physical examination and set up a schedule for vaccinations and other necessary wellness visits. Be sure to show your vet any health and inoculation records, which you should have received from your breeder. Your vet is a great source of canine health information, so be sure to ask questions and take notes. Creating a health journal for your puppy will make a handy reference for his wellness and any future health problems that may arise.

"Pleased to meet you," says the puppy Xanudu von Pfefferhauschen, owned by Nancy Holmes.

MEETING THE FAMILY

Your Affenpinscher's homecoming is an exciting time for all members of the family, and it's only natural that everyone will be eager to meet him, pet him and play with him. However, for the puppy's sake, it's best to make these initial family meetings as uneventful as possible so that the pup is not overwhelmed with too much too soon. Remember, he has just left his dam and his littermates and is away from the breeder's home for the first time. Also remember that the Affen takes time to warm up to new people, so don't rush it. Despite his fuzzy wagging tail, he is still apprehensive and wondering where he is and who all these strange humans are. It's best to let him explore on his own and meet the family members as he feels comfortable. Let him investigate all the new smells, sights and sounds at his own pace. Children should be especially careful to not get overly excited, use loud voices or hug the pup too tightly. Be calm, gentle and affectionate, and be ready to comfort him if he appears frightened or uneasy.

Be sure to show your puppy his new crate during this first day home. Toss a treat or two inside the crate; if he associates the crate with food, he will associate the crate with good things. If he is comfortable with the crate, you can offer him his first meal inside it. Leave the door ajar so he can wander in and out as he chooses.

PUPPY PARASITES

Parasites are nasty little critters that live in or on your dog or puppy. Most puppies are born with ascarid roundworms, which are acquired from dormant ascarids residing in the dam. Other parasites can be acquired through contact with infected fecal matter. Take a stool sample to your vet for testing. He will prescribe a safe wormer to treat any parasites found in your puppy's stool. Always have a fecal test performed at your puppy's annual veterinary exam.

FIRST NIGHT IN HIS NEW HOME

So much has happened in your Affenpinscher puppy's first day away from the breeder. He's had his first car ride to his new home. He's met his new human family and perhaps the other family pets. He has explored his new house and yard, at least those places where he is to be allowed during his first weeks at home. He may have visited his new veterinarian. He has eaten his first meal or two away from his dam and litter-mates. Surely that's enough to tire out a young Affenpinscher pup...or so you hope!

It's bedtime. During the day, the pup investigated his crate, which is his new den and sleeping space, so it is not entirely strange to him. Line the crate with a soft towel or blanket that he can snuggle into and gently place him into the crate for the night. Some breeders send home a piece of bedding from where the pup slept with his littermates, and those familiar scents are a great comfort for the puppy on his first night without his siblings.

He will probably whine or cry. The puppy is objecting to the confinement and the fact that he is alone for the first time. This can be a stressful time for you as well as for the pup. It's important that you remain strong and don't let the puppy out of his crate to comfort him. He will fall asleep

eventually. If you release him, the puppy will learn that crying means "out" and will continue that habit. You are laying the groundwork for future habits. Some breeders find that soft music can soothe a crying pup and help him get to sleep.

An excellent example of the belge color on a young puppy.

SOCIALIZING YOUR PUPPY

The first 20 weeks of your Affen-pinscher puppy's life are the most important of his entire lifetime. A properly socialized puppy will grow up to be a confident and stable adult who will be a pleas-ure to live with and a welcome addition to the neighborhood.

The importance of socializa-tion cannot be overemphasized. Research on canine behavior has proven that puppies who are not exposed to new sights, sounds, people and animals during their first 20 weeks of life will grow up

Affenpinschers usually get along well with other dogs with proper introductions and supervision. This Affen has enlisted a Boston Terrier pal's help with the gardening.

to be timid and fearful, even aggressive, and unable to flourish outside of their familiar home environment.

Socializing your puppy is not difficult and, in fact, will be a fun time for you both. Lead training goes hand in hand with socialization, so your puppy will be learning how to walk on a lead at the same time that he's meeting the neighborhood. Because the Affenpinscher is such a remarkable and interesting breed, everyone will want to meet "the new kid on the block." Keeping his wariness of strangers in mind, take him for short walks, to the park and to other dog-friendly places where he will encounter new people, especially children. Puppies automatically recognize children as "little people" and are drawn to play with them. Just make sure that you supervise these meetings

and that the children do not get too rough or encourage him to play too hard. An overzealous pup can often nip too hard, frightening the child and in turn making the puppy overly excited. A bad experience in puppyhood can impact a dog for life, so a pup that has a negative experience with a child may grow up to be shy or even aggressive around children. In fact, it's best to discourage unknown children or adults from just coming up and petting your Affenpinscher without a proper introduction. Sometimes meeting strangers on the street will upset or agitate your Affen.

Take your puppy along on your daily errands. Puppies are natural "people magnets," and most people who see your pup will want to pet him. All of these encounters will help to mold him into a confident adult dog. Likewise, you will soon feel like a confident, responsible dog owner, rightly proud of your handsome Affenpinscher.

Your Affen will go through his fear period, between eight and ten weeks of age, while still with the breeder. This is a serious imprinting period, and the breeder is careful that all of the pup's experiences during this time are gentle and positive. A frightening or negative event could leave a permanent impression that could affect his future behavior if a similar situation arises.

Also make sure that your puppy has received his first and second rounds of vaccinations before you expose him to other dogs or bring him to places that other dogs may frequent. Avoid dog parks and other strange-dog areas until your vet assures you that your puppy is fully immunized and resistant to the diseases that can be passed between canines. Discuss safe socialization with your vet and breeder, as some breeders recommend socializing the puppy even before he has received all of his inoculations, depending on how outgoing the puppy may be.

LEADER OF THE PUPPY'S PACK

Like other canines, your puppy needs an authority figure, someone he can look up to and regard as the leader of his "pack." His first pack leader was his dam, who taught him to be polite and not chew too hard on her ears or nip at her muzzle. He learned those same lessons from his littermates. If he played too rough, they cried in pain and stopped the game, which sent an important message to the rowdy puppy.

As puppies play together, they are also struggling to determine who will be the boss. Being pack animals, dogs need someone to be in charge. If a litter of puppies remained together beyond puppyhood, one of the pups would emerge as the strongest one, the

CONFINEMENT
It is wise to keep your puppy confined to a small "puppy-proofed" area of the house for his first few weeks at home. Gate or block off a space near the door he will use for outdoor potty trips. Expandable baby gates are useful to create your puppy's designated area. If he is allowed to roam through the entire house or even only several rooms, it will be more difficult to house-train him.

one who calls the shots.

Once your puppy leaves the pack, he will look intuitively for a new leader. If he does not recognize you as that leader, he will try to assume that position for himself. Of course, it is hard to imagine your monkey-faced

Affenpinschers of all ages welcome a comfy bed and a place to call their own.

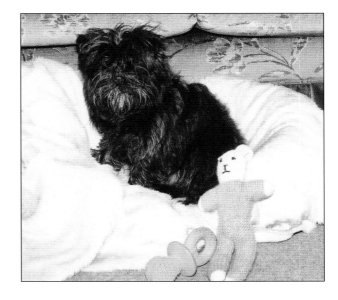

Affenpinscher puppy trying to be in charge when he is so small and seemingly helpless. You must remember that these are natural canine instincts. Do not cave in and allow your pup to get the upper "paw," because an Affen will certainly take advantage of the situation!

Just as socialization is so important during these first 20 weeks, so too is your puppy's early education. He was born without any bad habits. He does not know what is good or bad behavior. If he does things like nipping and digging, it's because he is having fun and doesn't know that humans consider these things as "bad." It's your job to teach him proper puppy manners, and this is the best time to accomplish that—before he has developed bad habits, since it is much more difficult to "unlearn" or correct unacceptable learned behavior than to

teach good behavior from the start.

Make sure that all members of the family understand the importance of being consistent when training their new puppy. If you tell the puppy to stay off the sofa and your daughter allows him to cuddle on the couch to watch her favorite television show, your pup will be confused about what he is and is not allowed to do. Have a family conference before your pup comes home so that everyone understands the basic principles of puppy training and the rules you have set forth for the pup and agrees to follow them.

The old saying that "an ounce of prevention is worth a pound of cure" is especially true when it comes to puppies. It is much easier to prevent inappropriate behavior than it is to change it. It's also easier and less stressful for the pup, since it will keep discipline to a minimum and create a more positive learning environment for him. That, in turn, will also be easier on you.

SOLVING PUPPY PROBLEMS

CHEWING AND NIPPING
Nipping at fingers and toes is normal puppy behavior. Chewing is also the way that puppies investigate their surroundings. However, you will have to teach your puppy that chewing anything other than his toys is not

Pups receive much valuable early socialization from their littermates, with whom they share everything.

acceptable. That won't happen overnight and at times puppy teeth will test your patience. However, if you allow nipping and chewing to continue, just think about the damage that a mature Affenpinscher can do with a full set of adult teeth. Terriers are known for their teeth!

Whenever your puppy nips your hand or fingers, cry out "Ouch!" in a loud voice, which should startle your puppy and stop him from nipping, even if only for a moment. Immediately distract him by offering a small treat or an appropriate toy for him to chew instead (which means having chew toys and puppy treats handy or in your pockets at all times). Praise him when he takes the toy and tell him what a good fellow he is. Praise is just as or even more important in puppy training as discipline and correction.

Puppies also tend to nip at children more often than adults, since they perceive little ones to

On the move! Affenpinscher pups are naturally curious creatures. Providing plenty of safe toys should help direct their energies in an appropriate way.

be more vulnerable and more similar to their littermates. Teach your children appropriate responses to nipping behavior. If they are unable to handle it themselves, you may have to intervene. Puppy nips can be quite painful and a child's frightened reaction will only encourage a puppy to nip harder, which is a natural canine response. As with all other puppy situations, interaction between your Affenpinscher puppy and children should be supervised.

Chewing on objects, not just family members' fingers and ankles, is also normal canine behavior that can be especially tedious (for the owner, not the pup) during the teething period when the puppy's adult teeth are coming in. At this stage, chewing

ESTABLISH A ROUTINE

Routine is very important to a puppy's learning environment. To facilitate house-training, use the same exit/entrance door for potty trips and always take the puppy to the same place in the yard. The same principle of consistency applies to all other aspects of puppy training.

just plain feels good. Furniture legs and cabinet corners are common puppy favorites. Shoes and other personal items also taste pretty good to a pup.

The best solution is, once again, prevention. If you value something, keep it tucked away and out of reach. You can't hide your dining-room table in a closet, but you can try to deflect the chewing by applying a bitter product made just to deter dogs from chewing. Available in a spray or cream, this substance is vile-tasting, although safe for dogs, and most puppies will avoid the forbidden object after one tiny taste. You also can apply the product to your leash if the puppy tries to chew on it during leash-training sessions.

Keep a ready supply of safe chews handy to offer your Affenpinscher as a distraction when he starts to chew on something that's a "no-no." Remember, at this tender age he does not yet know what is permitted or forbidden, so you have to be "on call" every minute he's awake and on the prowl.

You may lose a treasure or two during your puppy's growing-up period, and the furniture could sustain a nasty nick or two. These can be trying times, so be prepared for those inevitable accidents and comfort yourself in knowing that this too shall pass.

PUPPY WHINING

Puppies often cry and whine, just as infants and little children do. It's their way of telling us that they are lonely or in need of attention. Your puppy will miss his littermates and will feel insecure when he is left alone. You may be out of the house or just in another room, but he will still feel alone. During these times, the puppy's crate should be his personal comfort station, a place all his own where he can feel safe and secure. Once he learns that being alone is okay and not something to be feared, he will settle down without crying or objecting. You might want to leave a radio on while he is crated, as the sound of human voices can be soothing and will give the impression that people are around.

Give your puppy a favorite long-lasting toy to entertain him whenever he is crated. You will both be happier: the puppy because he is safe in his den and you because he is quiet, safe and not getting into puppy escapades that can wreak havoc in your house or cause him danger.

To make sure that your puppy will always view his crate as a safe and cozy place, never, ever use the crate as punishment. That's the best way to turn the crate into a negative place that the pup will want to avoid. Sure, you can use the crate for your own peace of mind if your puppy is getting into trouble and needs some "time out." Just don't let him know that! Never scold the pup and immediately place him into the crate. Count to ten, give him a hug and maybe a treat, then scoot him into his crate.

It's also important not to make a big fuss when he is released from the crate. That will make getting out of the crate more appealing than being in the crate, which is just the opposite of what you are trying to achieve.

FOOD GUARDING

Some dogs are picky eaters; others seem to inhale their food without chewing it. Occasionally the true "chow hound" will become protective of his food, which is one dangerous step toward other aggressive behavior. Food guarding is obvious: your puppy will growl, snarl or even attempt to bite you if you approach his food bowl or put your hand into his dish while he's eating.

This behavior is not acceptable and very preventable! If your puppy is an especially voracious eater, sit next to him occasionally while he eats and dangle your fingers in his food bowl. Don't feed him in a corner, where he could feel possessive of his eating space. Rather, place

his food bowl in an open area of your kitchen where you are in close proximity. Occasionally remove his food in mid-meal, tell him he's a good boy and return his bowl.

If your pup becomes possessive of his food, look for other signs of future aggression, like guarding his favorite toys or refusing to obey obedience commands that he knows. Consult an obedience trainer for help in reinforcing obedience so your Affenpinscher will fully understand that *you* are the boss.

The crate is an invaluable tool from puppyhood through adulthood. It provides a sense of security for both Affenpinscher and owner: he has his own "den" and you know that he is safe there.

PROPER CARE OF YOUR

AFFENPINSCHER

FEEDING

Feeding your dog the best diet is based on various factors, including age, activity level, overall condition and size of breed. When you visit the breeder, he will share with you his advice about the proper diet for your dog based on his experience with the breed and the foods with which he has had success. Likewise, your vet will be a helpful source of advice throughout the dog's life and will aid you in planning a diet for optimal health.

FEEDING THE PUPPY

Of course, your pup's very first food will be his dam's milk. There may be special situations in which pups fail to nurse, necessitating that the breeder hand-feed them with a formula, but for the most part pups spend the first weeks of life nursing from their dam. The breeder weans the pups by gradually introducing solid foods and decreasing the milk meals. Pups may even start themselves off on the weaning process, albeit inadvertently, if they snatch bites from their mom's food bowl.

By the time the pups are ready for new homes, they are fully weaned and eating a good puppy food. As a new owner, you may be thinking, "Great! The breeder has taken care of the hard part." Not so fast.

A puppy's first year of life is the time when all or most of his growth and development takes place. This is a delicate time, and diet plays a huge role in proper skeletal and muscular formation. Improper diet and exercise habits can lead to damaging problems that will compromise the dog's health and movement for his entire life. That being said, new owners should not worry needlessly. With the myriad types of food formulated specifically for growing pups of different-sized breeds, dog-food manufacturers have taken much of the guesswork out of feeding your puppy well. Since growth-food formulas are designed to provide the nutrition that a growing puppy needs, it is unnecessary and, in fact, can prove harmful to add supplements to the diet. Research has shown that too much of certain vitamin supplements and minerals predispose a dog to skeletal problems. It's by no means a case of "if a little is good, a lot is better." At every stage of your dog's life, too much or too little in the way of nutrients can be harmful, which is why a manufactured complete food is the easiest way to know that your dog is getting what he needs.

Because of a young pup's small body and accordingly small digestive system, his daily portion will be divided up into small meals throughout the day. This can mean starting off with three or more meals a day and decreasing the number of meals as the pup

matures to a twice-daily schedule. Also, Affens do best on "small bite" food as pups and adults. At around 9–12 months, you can switch to an adult food.

Regarding the feeding schedule, feeding the pup at the same times and in the same place each day is important for both housebreaking purposes and establishing the dog's everyday routine. As for the amount to feed, growing puppies generally need proportionately more food per body weight than their adult counterparts, but a pup should never be allowed to gain excess weight. Dogs of all ages should be kept in proper body condition, but extra weight can strain a pup's developing frame, causing skeletal problems.

A quality food formulated for his stage in life and a constant supply of fresh water should be all you need to maintain a healthy Affenpinscher.

NOT HUNGRY?

No dog in his right mind would turn down his dinner, would he? If you notice that your dog has lost interest in his food, there could be any number of causes. Dental problems are a common cause of appetite loss, one that is often overlooked. If your dog has a toothache, a loose tooth or sore gums from infection, chances are it doesn't feel so good to chew. Think about when you've had a toothache! If your dog does not approach the food bowl with his usual enthusiasm, look inside his mouth for signs of a problem. Whatever the cause, you'll want to consult your vet so that your chow hound can get back to his happy, hungry self as soon as possible.

Watch your pup's weight as he grows and, if the recommended amounts seem to be too much or too little for your pup, consult the vet about appropriate dietary changes. Keep in mind that treats, although small, can quickly add up throughout the day, contributing unnecessary calories. Treats are fine when used prudently; opt for dog treats specially formulated to be healthy or for nutritious snacks like small pieces of cheese or cooked chicken. Crunchy biscuits can be used as teething aids.

FEEDING THE ADULT DOG

For the adult (meaning physically mature) dog, feeding properly is about maintenance, not growth. Again, correct weight is a concern. Your dog should appear fit and should have an evident "waist." His ribs should not be protruding (a sign of being underweight), but they should be covered by only a slight layer of fat. Under normal circumstances, an adult dog can be maintained fairly easily with a high-quality nutritionally complete adult-formula food.

Factor treats into your dog's overall daily caloric intake, and avoid offering table scraps. Over-weight dogs are more prone to health problems. Research has even shown that obesity takes years off a dog's life. With that in mind, resist the urge to overfeed and over-treat. Don't make unnec-essary additions to your dog's diet, whether with tidbits or with extra vitamins and minerals.

The amount of food needed for proper maintenance will vary depending on the individual dog's activity level, but you will be able to tell whether the daily portions are keeping him in good shape. With the wide variety of good complete foods available, choos-ing what to feed is largely a matter of personal preference. Just as with the puppy, the adult dog should have consistency in his mealtimes and feeding place. In addition to a consistent routine, regular mealtimes also allow the owner to see how much his dog is eating. If the dog seems never to be satisfied or, likewise, becomes uninterested in his food, the owner will know right away that something is wrong and can consult the vet.

In general, Affenpinschers are

Water should be available to the Affenpinscher at all times, indoors and out, so that he can quench his thirst whenever he needs to.

DON'T OVERFEED
One problem for the new owner may be the tendency to overfeed his pet. The older Affenpinscher loves to eat. Obesity will tend to shorten his life span. With adequate food and care the active, healthy Affenpinscher will generally live to between 12 and 16 years of age.

---

not picky eaters. In fact, they love to eat so much that you must be careful to limit the quantities you feed so that they do not become overweight. If you have more than one pet, it is important to feed them in such a way that they are not tempted to steal each other's food, both because your Affenpinscher is likely to be very territorial about his food bowl and because he could easily put on extra weight. Also, never feed your Affenpinscher from the table or the dog will become a real pest.

Table scraps and sudden dietary changes are not recommended at any age, as they may cause stomach upset or create finicky eaters. Among the foods to particularly avoid are soft bones, which may splinter and cause severe internal damage, and chocolate, nuts, onions, grapes and raisins, all of which are highly poisonous to all dogs.

As the Affenpinscher's skin tends to be dry, particularly in overheated homes, the addition of a skin and coat supplement to your dog's diet will help keep his coat glossy and his skin soft and healthy; ask your vet to suggest something suitable. If your Affenpinscher develops health problems, particularly in old age, your vet may recommend a special diet.

DIETS FOR THE AGING DOG

A good rule of thumb is that once a dog has reached 75% of his expected lifespan, he has reached "senior citizen" or geriatric status. Your Affenpinscher will be considered a senior at about 9 years of age; he has a projected lifespan of between 12 and 16 years. (The smallest breeds generally enjoy the longest lives and the largest breeds the shortest.)

What does aging have to do with your dog's diet? No, he won't get a discount at the local diner's early-bird special. Yes, he will require some dietary changes to accommodate the changes that come along with increased age. One change is that the older dog's dietary needs become more similar to that of a puppy. Specifically, dogs can metabolize more protein as youngsters and seniors than in the adult-maintenance stage. Discuss with your vet whether you need to switch to a higher-protein or senior-formulated food or whether your current adult-dog food contains sufficient nutrition for the senior.

Too much exercise could cause your young Affenpinscher injury. Don't worry, normal puppy activities will keep him fit.

Watching the dog's weight remains essential, even more so in the senior stage. Older dogs are already more vulnerable to illness, and obesity only contributes to their susceptibility to problems. As the older dog becomes less active and thus exercises less, his regular portions may cause him to gain weight. At this point, you may consider decreasing his daily food intake or switching to a reduced-calorie food. As with other changes, you should consult your vet for advice.

WATER

Just as your dog needs proper nutrition from his food, water is an essential "nutrient" as well. Water keeps the dog's body properly hydrated and promotes normal function of the body's systems. During house-training, it is necessary to keep an eye on how much water your Affenpinscher is drinking, but once he is reliably trained he should have access to clean fresh water at all times, especially if you feed dry food. Make certain that the dog's water bowl is clean, and change the water often.

EXERCISING YOUR AFFENPINSCHER

Your Affenpinscher is small, playful and active enough to be able to get sufficient physical exercise within the confines of your home. As this is a dog that uses his front paws like hands, do not be surprised to see your pet exercise himself by tossing and chasing his toys. Even though the Affenpinscher does not require a great deal of physical activity, he enjoys a brisk daily walk (or two) and has the stamina to join you on hikes, during which his natural curiosity about the world will be appeased momentarily. Your pet will also enjoy outside playtime in a securely fenced yard. Any exercise out in the open requires your Affen to be on his leash.

GROOMING YOUR AFFEN

The Affenpinscher does not need much grooming. Because of its hard terrier-like coat, it doesn't become easily matted or tangled. Weekly brushing and a combing out of the furnishing on the legs and head will maintain its typical scruffy appearance. There is some shedding of the undercoat, but the weekly maintenance will control this. The head and facial hair can become sticky depending on the consistency of food. Regular cleaning of the face with a damp wash cloth and a comb after eating will prevent a messy mustache and beard.

A monthly bath, toenail clipping and trimming of the hair on the rear, tail and feet will help to keep the dog neat and clean. Trim the hair on the ears. Also pull the

The Affenpinscher's unique facial furnishings require special attention to keep them tangle-free and tidy.

hair out of the inside of the ears. The head and face of this breed are unique, and the hair should stand off from them. Some care should be taken to trim the hair on the face so that the eyes can be seen. With scissors, layer the hair to a length from about three-quarters of an inch to an inch and a half starting at the nose and going up to just behind the ears. Keep in mind that you are trying to create the image of a pom-pom chrysanthemum. Carefully cut the hair short on the top of the muzzle and near the inside corners of the eyes. Keep the hair on top of the head just a bit longer than the tip or top of the ears. Be careful so as not to nick the ears while using the scissors. Some plucking or hand pulling of the long coat hair is needed to maintain the hard texture and manageable coat length.

PUPPY STEPS

Puppies are brimming with activity and enthusiasm. It seems that they can play all day and night without tiring, but don't overdo your puppy's exercise regimen. Easy does it for the puppy's first six to nine months. Keep walks brief and don't let the puppy engage in stressful jumping games. The puppy frame is delicate, and too much exercise during those critical growing months can cause injury to his bone structure, ligaments and musculature. Save his first jog for his first birthday!

LEFT: After a thorough brushing, combing through the coat will remove any remaining tangles.
RIGHT: Don't forget the hard-to-reach places, being especially careful in these sensitive areas.

LEFT: The tail can be tidied up by trimming off excess hair with scissors.
RIGHT: Use grooming time to check your Affen's teeth and mouth, and brush his teeth at least weekly, daily if possible. Use a toothbrush and toothpaste made for dogs.

The areas around the eyes should be cleaned daily. To prevent eye problems, you may wish to pluck with your thumb and finger any hairs at the inside corners of the eyes that are touching the eyes. This hair should not be cut with scissors, as this creates short hairs that rub and irritate the eyes. The eyebrows should be combed forward and scissored short enough so that they do not obscure the dog's vision. The hair on the top of the head may or may not be trimmed, and the hair on the sides of the face from the outside of the eyes may be shortened to blend with the neck hair. This enhances the dome of the skull and helps to create the desired monkey-like expression.

For appearance's sake, you may use scissors to trim excess hair overhanging the edges of the ears; trim longer hair off the ears themselves and all sides of the tail for a smooth, pleasing look; round the feet for neatness; and trim the hair between the pads of the feet. You may also wish to clip the stomach hair with a #10 blade, particularly to prevent odor on a male.

On a mature dog, the hair will not all be of the same length. It will be naturally longer over the neck and chest and on the head and lower legs. Excessive hair over the hindquarters on a pet Affenpinscher with a profuse coat may be clipped, as is often done with schnauzers, but a clipper is generally not used on a show dog, as it destroys the proper harsh texture of the coat and may change the color as well.

Many pet owners will have their Affenpinschers groomed professionally every six to ten weeks. This may include a clip-down, but each owner needs to

---

SCOOTING HIS BOTTOM

Here's a doggy problem that many owners tend to neglect. If your dog is scooting his rear end around the carpet, he probably is experiencing anal-sac impaction or blockage. The anal sacs are the two grape-sized glands on either side of the dog's vent. The dog cannot empty these glands, which become filled with a foul-smelling material. The dog may attempt to lick the area to relieve the pressure. He may also rub his anus on your walls, furniture or floors.

Don't neglect your dog's rear end during grooming sessions. By squeezing both sides of the anus with a soft cloth, you can express some of the material in the sacs. If the material is pasty and thick, you likely will need the assistance of a veterinarian. Vets know how to express the glands and can show you how to do it correctly without hurting the dog or spraying yourself with the unpleasant liquid.

Trimming around the feet results in a tidy look.

decide on the "look" he prefers and discuss this with the groomer. Regular brushing and trimming can keep the need for professional help to a minimum. A bristle brush, a slicker brush, a metal comb, a flea comb, a small dog toenail cutter, thinning shears and a pair of small sharp scissors with rounded points is the equipment you will need to keep your pet neat and clean.

The show dog will need more hand stripping and trimming by someone with the knowledge of appropriate show grooming. One of the major differences between the older style and the modern Affenpinscher is in the appearance of the show dogs. The top-winning contemporary Affenpinschers are more precisely shaped with tighter, shorter coats.

BATHING

If groomed and tidied up regularly, an Affenpinscher will need bathing only occasionally for healthy skin and a healthy, shiny coat. Bathing is seldom required if the entire body is brushed regularly, but a damp cloth may be used to remove dirt or anything sticky in the coat that cannot be removed with a brush. If you give your dog his first bath when he is young, he will become accustomed to the process. Wrestling a dog into the tub or chasing a freshly shampooed dog who has escaped from the bath will be no fun. Most dogs don't naturally enjoy their baths, but you at least

WATER SHORTAGE

No matter how well behaved your dog is, bathing is always a project! Nothing can substitute for a good warm bath, but owners do have the option of giving their dogs "dry" baths. Pet shops sell excellent products, in both powder and spray forms, designed for spot-cleaning your dog. These dry shampoos are convenient for touch-up jobs when you don't have the time to bathe your dog in the traditional way.

Muddy feet, messy behinds and smelly coats can be spot-cleaned and deodorized with a "wet-nap"-style cleaner. On those days when your dog insists on rolling in fresh goose droppings and there's no time for a bath, a spot bath can save the day. These pre-moistened wipes are also handy for other grooming needs like wiping faces, ears and eyes and freshening tails and behinds.

want yours to cooperate with you.

Before bathing the dog, have the items you'll need close at hand. First, decide where you will bathe the dog. You should have a tub or basin with a non-slip surface. Affenpinschers can even be bathed in a sink. In warm weather, some like to use a portable pool in the yard, although you'll want to make sure your dog doesn't head for the nearest dirt pile following his bath! You will also need a hose or shower spray to wet the coat thoroughly, a shampoo formulated for dogs, absorbent towels and perhaps a blow dryer. Human shampoos are too harsh for dogs' coats and will dry them out.

Before wetting the dog, give him a brush-through to remove any dead hair, dirt and mats. Make sure he is at ease in the tub and have the water at a comfortable temperature. Begin bathing by wetting the coat all the way down to the skin. Massage in the shampoo, keeping it away from his face and eyes. Rinse him thoroughly, again avoiding the eyes and ears, as you don't want to get water into the ear canals. A thorough rinsing is important, as shampoo residue is drying and itchy to the dog. After rinsing, wrap him in a towel to absorb the initial moisture. You can finish drying with either a towel or a blow dryer on low heat, held at a safe distance from the dog. You should keep the dog

indoors and away from drafts until he is completely dry.

NAIL CLIPPING

Having their nails trimmed is not on many dogs' lists of favorite things to do. With this in mind, you will need to accustom your puppy to the procedure at a young age so that he will sit still (well, as still as he can) for his pedicures. Long nails can cause the dog's feet to spread, which is not good for him; likewise, long nails can hurt if they unintentionally scratch, not good for you.

Some dogs' nails are worn down naturally by regular walking on hard surfaces, so the frequency with which you clip depends on your individual dog. Look at his nails from time to time and clip as needed; a good way to know when it's time for a trim is if you hear your dog clicking as he walks across the floor.

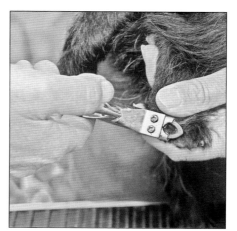

Trim the nails regularly. Use nail clippers for dogs, like the guillotine-type shown here.

There are several types of nail clippers and even electric nail-grinding tools made for dogs. First we'll discuss using the clipper. To start, have your clipper ready and some doggie treats on hand. You want your pup to view his nail-clipping sessions in a positive light, and what better way to convince him than with food?

EYE CARE

During grooming sessions, pay extra attention to the condition of your dog's eyes. If the area around the eyes is soiled or if tear staining has occurred, there are various cleaning agents made especially for this purpose. Look at the dog's eyes to make sure no debris has entered; dogs with large eyes and those who spend time outdoors are especially prone to this. Pluck any hairs that may be irritating the eyes.

The signs of an eye infection are obvious: mucus, redness, puffiness, scabs or other signs of irritation. If your dog's eyes become infected, the vet will likely prescribe an antibiotic ointment for treatment. If you notice signs of more serious problems, such as opacities in the eye, which usually indicate cataracts, consult the vet at once. Taking time to pay attention to your dog's eyes will alert you in the early stages of any problem so that you can get your dog treatment as soon as possible. You could save your dog's sight!

You may want to enlist the help of an assistant to comfort the pup and offer treats as you concentrate on the clipping itself. The guillotine-type clipper is thought of by many as the easiest type to use; the nail tip is inserted into the opening, and blades on the top and bottom snip it off in one clip.

Start by grasping the pup's paw; a little pressure on the foot pad causes the nail to extend, making it easier to clip. Clip off a little at a time. If you can see the "quick," which is a blood vessel that runs through each nail, you will know how much to trim, as you do not want to cut into the quick. On that note, if you do cut the quick, which will cause bleeding, you can stem the flow of blood with a styptic pencil or other clotting agent. If you mistakenly nip the quick, do not panic or fuss, as this will cause the pup to be afraid. Simply reassure the pup, stop the bleeding and move on to the next nail. Don't be discouraged; you will become a professional canine pedicurist with practice.

You may or may not be able to see the quick, so it's best to just clip off a small bit at a time. If you see a dark dot in the center of the nail, this is the quick and your cue to stop clipping. Tell the puppy he's a "good boy" and offer a piece of treat with each nail. You can also use nail-clipping time to examine the footpads,

making sure that they are not dry and cracked and that nothing has become embedded in them.

The nail grinder, the other choice, is many owners' first choice. Accustoming the puppy to the sound of the grinder and sensation of the buzz presents fewer challenges than the clipper, and there's no chance of cutting through the quick. You must, however, be careful not to catch any of the coat in the grinder. Use the grinder on a low setting and always talk soothingly to your dog. He won't mind his salon visit, and he'll have nicely polished nails as well.

EAR CLEANING

Keep the Affenpinscher's ears clean by using a cotton ball and ear powder made especially for dogs. Additionally, you will want to pluck any excess hairs from the ears that might cause the dog irritation. Do not probe into the ear canal with a cotton ball, as this

can cause injury. Be on the lookout for any signs of infection or ear-mite infestation. If your Affenpinscher has been shaking his head or scratching at his ears frequently, this usually indicates a problem. If the dog's ears have an unusual odor, this is a sure sign of mite infestation or infection, and a signal to have his ears checked by the veterinarian.

ID FOR YOUR DOG

You love your Affenpinscher and want to keep him safe. Of course you take every precaution to prevent his escaping from the yard or becoming lost or stolen. You have a sturdy high fence and you always keep your dog on lead when out and about in public places. If your dog is not properly identified, however, you are overlooking a major aspect of his safety. We hope to never be in a situation where our dog is missing, but we should practice

The outer ear is cleaned with a soft cotton wipe and ear-cleaning powder or liquid.

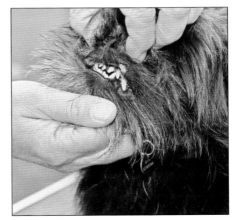

Toy breeds are known to have problems with their teeth. Incorporate your home dental-care regimen into your grooming routine.

prevention in the unfortunate case that this happens; identification greatly increases the chances of your dog's being returned to you.

There are several ways to identify your dog. First, the traditional dog tag should be a staple in your dog's wardrobe, attached to his everyday collar. Tags can be made of sturdy plastic and various metals and should include your contact information so that a person who finds the dog can get in touch with you right away to arrange his return. Many people today enjoy the wide range of decorative tags available, so have fun and create a tag to match your dog's personality. Of course, it is important that the tag stays on the collar, so have a secure "O" ring attachment; you also can explore the type of tag that slides right

CAR CAUTION

You may like to bring your canine companion along on the daily errands, but if you will be running in and out from place to place and can't bring him indoors with you, leave him at home. Your dog should never be left alone in the car, not even for a minute—*never!* A car heats up very quickly, and even a cracked-open window will not help. In fact, leaving the window cracked will be dangerous if the dog becomes uncomfortable and tries to escape. When in doubt, leave your dog home, where you know he will be safe.

onto the collar. A collar and tags signify that a dog is someone's pet, making it more likely that someone will help your dog if he gets away from you.

In addition to the ID tag, which every dog should wear even if identified by another method, two other forms of identification have become popular: microchipping and tattooing. In microchipping, a tiny scannable chip is painlessly inserted under the dog's skin. The number is registered to you so that, if your lost dog turns up at a clinic or shelter, the chip can be scanned to retrieve your contact information.

The advantage of the microchip is that it is a permanent form of ID, but there are some factors to consider. Several different companies make microchips, and not all are compatible with the others' scanning devices. It's best to find a company with a universal microchip that can be read by scanners made by other companies as well. It won't do any good to have the dog chipped if the information cannot be retrieved. Also, not every humane society, shelter and clinic is equipped with a scanner, although more and more facilities are equipping themselves. In fact, many shelters microchip dogs that they adopt out to new homes.

In the US, there are five or six major microchip manufacturers as well as a few databases. The

If given the choice, your Affenpinscher would be in the driver's seat!

American Kennel Club's Companion Animal Recovery unit works in conjunction with HomeAgain™ Companion Animal Retrieval System (Schering-Plough). In the UK, The Kennel Club is affiliated with the National Pet Register, operated by Wood Green Animal Shelters.

Because the microchip is not visible to the eye, the dog must wear a tag that states that he is microchipped so that whoever picks him up will know to have him scanned. He of course also should have a tag with contact information in case his chip cannot be read. Humane societies and veterinary clinics offer microchipping service, which is usually very affordable.

Though less popular than microchipping, tattooing is another permanent method of ID for dogs. Most vets perform this service, and there are also clinics that perform dog tattooing. This is also an affordable procedure and one that will not cause much discomfort for the dog. It is best to put the tattoo in a visible area, such as inside the ear flap, to deter theft. It is sad to say that there are cases of dogs' being stolen and sold to research laboratories, but such laboratories will not accept tattooed dogs.

To ensure that the tattoo is effective in aiding your dog's return to you, the tattoo number must be registered with a national organization. That way, when someone finds a tattooed dog, a phone call to the registry will quickly match the dog with his owner.

If you are looking for a dog that is easy to train, a pleasure in obedience class and a "snap" to work with in obedience shows and agility trials, then the Affenpinscher is definitely not your dog. The energetic "monkey terrier" has a bit of a stubborn streak, highlighted by a somewhat perverse sense of humor. Indeed, training an actual monkey would be much simpler than taking on the Affenpinscher.

"SCHOOL" MODE

When is your puppy ready for a lesson? Maybe not always when you are. Attempting training with treats just before his mealtime is asking for disaster. Notice what times of day he performs best and make that Fido's school time.

Nonetheless, do not lose heart, because the Affenpinscher can be bribed! Obedience training an Affen revolves around delicious tidbits and profuse praise. Affens like to be rewarded for condescending to human training games, and these independent thinkers will perform your command twice (but the third time is silly repetition and not very likely).

To rear a companion dog, all agree, training is absolutely essential, so we begin our upward battle of educating your beloved Affenpinscher. Of course, to train any dog is a big responsibility and, if not trained sensibly, your otherwise delightful companion may develop unacceptable behav-

Whether yours is a show puppy or simply a home companion, every Affenpinscher requires obedience training. Show puppies learn to stand and stay from the time they are ten weeks of age.

ior that annoys you or could even cause family friction.

As long as you don't mind being with the class clown, the smartest fellow in the group, enrolling in an obedience class might be a good idea. Having a professional trainer available to you as you teach your Affen good manners can only help the situation. Plus, you can learn how and why he behaves the way he does, provided the obedience instructor has experience working with "somewhat difficult" students.

There's a big difference between training an adult dog and training a young puppy. With a young puppy, everything is new. At twelve weeks of age, he will be experiencing many things, and he has nothing with which to compare these experiences. Up to this point, he has been with his dam and littermates, not one-on-

one with people except in his interactions with his breeder and visitors to the litter.

When you first bring the puppy home, he is eager to please you. This means that he accepts doing things your way. During the next couple of months, he will absorb the basis of everything he needs to know for the rest of his life. This early age is even referred to as the "sponge" stage. After that, for the next 18 months, it's up to you to reinforce good manners by building on the foundation that you've established. Once your puppy is reliable in basic commands and behavior and has reached the appropriate age, you may gradually introduce him to some of the interesting sports, games and activities available to pet owners and their dogs.

With an intelligent expression and a twinkle in his eye, the Affenpinscher can be a challenging yet entertaining breed to train.

LEADER OF THE PACK

Canines are pack animals. They live according to pack rules, and every pack has only one leader. Guess what? That's you! To establish your position of authority, lay down the rules and be fair and good-natured in all of your dealings with your dog. He will consider young children as his littermates, but the one who trains him, who feeds him, who grooms him, who expects him to come into line, that's his leader. And he who leads must be obeyed.

Raising your puppy is a family affair. Each member of the family must know what rules to set forth for the puppy and how to use the same one-word commands to mean exactly the same thing every time. Even if yours is a large family, one person will soon be considered by the pup to be the leader, the alpha person in his pack, the "boss" who must be obeyed. Often that highly regarded person turns out to be the one who feeds the puppy. Food ranks very high on the

puppy's list of important things! That's why your puppy is rewarded with small treats along with verbal praise when he responds to you correctly. As the puppy learns to do what you want him to do, the food rewards are gradually eliminated and only the praise remains. If you were to keep up with the food treats, you could have two problems on your hands—an obese dog and a beggar.

Training begins the minute your Affenpinscher puppy steps through the doorway of your home, so don't make the mistake of putting the puppy on the floor and telling him by your actions to "Go for it! Run wild!" Even if this is your first puppy, you must act as if you know what you're doing: be the boss. An uncertain pup may be terrified to move, while a bold one will be ready to take you at your word and start plotting to destroy the house! Before you collected your puppy, you decided where his own special place would be, and that's where to put him when you first arrive home. Give him a house tour after he has investigated his area and had a nap and a bathroom "pit stop."

It's worth mentioning here that, if you've adopted an adult dog that is completely trained to your liking, lucky you! You're off the hook. However, if that dog spent his life up to this point in a

BREAKFAST NOOK

Mealtime should be a peaceful time for your puppy. Do not put his food and water bowls in a high-traffic area of the house. For example, give him an open area of the kitchen where he can eat undisturbed but where he will not be underfoot. Do not allow small children or other family members to disturb the pup when he is eating.

kennel, or even in a good home but without any real training, be prepared to tackle the job ahead. A dog three years of age or older with no previous training cannot be blamed for not knowing what he was never taught. While the dog is trying to understand and learn your rules, at the same time he has to unlearn many of his previously self-taught habits and general view of the world.

Working with a professional trainer will speed up your progress with an adopted adult dog. You'll need patience, too. Some new rules may be close to impossible for the dog to accept. After all, he's been successful so far by doing everything his way! (Patience again.) He may agree with your instruction for a few days and then slip back into his

When it's time to "go," it's time to go! This lucky Affen has his own doggie door with access to the fenced yard.

old ways, so you must be just as consistent and understanding in your teaching as you would be with a puppy. (More patience needed yet again.) Your dog has to learn to pay attention to your voice, your family, the daily routine, new smells, new sounds and, in some cases, even a new climate.

One of the most important things to find out about a newly

BASIC PRINCIPLES OF DOG TRAINING

1. Start training early. A young puppy is ready, willing and able.
2. Timing is your all-important tool. Praise at the exact time that the dog responds correctly. Pay close attention.
3. Patience is almost as important as timing!
4. Repeat! The same word has to mean the same thing every time.
5. In the beginning, praise all correct behavior verbally, along with treats and petting.

Despite your efforts to provide your puppy with chew toys, most pups can't resist the urge to nip at your shoes.

adopted adult dog is his reaction to children (yours and others), strangers and your friends, and how he acts upon meeting other dogs. If he was not socialized with dogs as a puppy, this could be a major problem. This does not mean that he's a "bad" dog, a vicious dog or an aggressive dog; rather, it means that he has no idea how to read another dog's body language. There's no way for him to tell whether the other dog is a friend or foe. Survival instinct takes over, telling him to attack first and ask questions later. This definitely calls for professional help and, even then, may not be a behavior that can be corrected 100% reliably (or even at all). If you have a puppy, this is why it is so very important to introduce your young puppy properly to other puppies and "dog-friendly" adult dogs.

BE UPSTANDING!

You are the dog's leader. During training, stand up straight so your dog looks up at you, and therefore up *to* you. Say the command words distinctly, in a clear, declarative tone of voice. (No barking!) Give rewards only as the correct response takes place (remember your timing!). Praise, smiles and treats are "rewards" used to positively reinforce correct responses. Don't repeat a mistake. Just change to another exercise—you will soon find success!

CANINE DEVELOPMENT SCHEDULE

It is important to understand how and at what age a puppy develops into adulthood. If you are a puppy owner, consult this Canine Development Schedule to determine the stage of development your puppy is currently experiencing. This knowledge will help you as you work with the puppy in the weeks and months ahead.

PERIOD	AGE	CHARACTERISTICS
FIRST TO THIRD	BIRTH TO SEVEN WEEKS	Puppy needs food, sleep and warmth and responds to simple and gentle touching. Needs mother for security and disciplining. Needs littermates for learning and interacting with other dogs. Pup learns to function within a pack and learns pack order of dominance. Begin socializing pup with adults and children for short periods. Pup begins to become aware of his environment.
FOURTH	EIGHT TO TWELVE WEEKS	Brain is fully developed. Pup needs socializing with outside world. Remove from mother and littermates. Needs to change from canine pack to human pack. Human dominance necessary. Fear period occurs between 8 and 12 weeks. Avoid fright and pain.
FIFTH	THIRTEEN TO SIXTEEN WEEKS	Training and formal obedience should begin. Less association with other dogs, more with people, places, situations. Period will pass easily if you remember this is pup's change-to-adolescence time. Be firm and fair. Flight instinct prominent. Permissiveness and over-disciplining can do permanent damage. Praise for good behavior.
JUVENILE	FOUR TO EIGHT MONTHS	Another fear period about seven to eight months of age. It passes quickly, but be cautious of fright and pain. Sexual maturity reached. Dominant traits established. Dog should understand sit, down, come and stay by now.

NOTE: THESE ARE APPROXIMATE TIME FRAMES. ALLOW FOR INDIVIDUAL DIFFERENCES IN PUPPIES.

After all, no dog likes harsh or inhumane methods, and the Affenpinscher is particularly sensitive to harsh corrections. You will likely ruin your dog (as well as your chances of training him) by losing your temper and resorting to unkind methods. All canines, and Affenpinschers in particular, respond favorably to gentle motivational methods and sincere praise and encouragement. Now let us get started.

HOUSE-TRAINING YOUR AFFENPINSCHER

Dogs are tactility-oriented when it comes to house-training. In other words, they respond to the surface on which they are given approval to eliminate. The choice is yours (the dog's version is in parentheses): The lawn (including the neighbors' lawns)? A bare patch of earth under a tree (where people like to sit and relax in the summertime)? Concrete steps or patio (all sidewalks, garages and basement floors)? The curbside (watch out for cars)? A small area of crushed stone in a corner of the yard (mine!)? The latter is the best choice if you can manage it, because it will remain strictly for the dog's use and is easy to keep clean.

You can start out with paper-training indoors and switch over to an outdoor surface as the puppy matures and gains control over his need to eliminate. For the nay-sayers, don't worry—this won't mean that the dog will soil on every piece of newspaper lying around the house. You are training him to go outside, remember? Starting out by paper-training often is the only choice for a city dog.

WHEN YOUR PUPPY'S "GOT TO GO"
Your puppy's need to relieve himself is seemingly non-stop, but signs of improvement will be seen each week. When you first bring him home, the puppy will have to be taken outside every time he wakes up, about 10–15 minutes after every meal and after every period of play—all day long, from first thing in the morning until his bedtime! That's a total of ten or more trips per day to teach the puppy where it's okay to relieve himself. With that schedule in

I WILL FOLLOW YOU
Obedience isn't just a classroom activity. In your home you have many great opportunities to teach your dog polite manners. Allowing your pet on the bed or furniture elevates him to your level, which is not a good idea (the word is "Off!"). Use the "umbilical cord" method, keeping your dog on lead so he has to go with you wherever you go. You sit, he sits. You walk, he heels. You stop, he sit-stays. Everywhere you go, he's with you, but you go first!

mind, you can see that house-training a young puppy is not a part-time job. It requires someone to be home all day.

If that seems overwhelming or impossible, do a little planning. For example, plan to pick up your puppy at the start of a vacation period. If you can't get home in the middle of the day, plan to hire a dog-sitter or ask a neighbor to come over to take the pup outside, feed him his lunch and then take him out again about ten or so minutes after he's eaten. Also make arrangements with that or another person to be your "emergency" contact if you have to stay late on the job. Remind yourself—repeatedly—that this hectic schedule improves as the puppy gets older.

HOME WITHIN A HOME

Your Affenpinscher puppy needs to be confined to one secure, puppy-proof area when no one is able to watch his every move. Generally the kitchen is the place of choice because the floor is washable. Likewise, it's a busy family area that will accustom the pup to a variety of noises, everything from pots and pans to the telephone, blender and dishwasher. He will also be enchanted by the smell of your cooking (and will never be critical when you burn something). An exercise pen (also called an "ex-pen," a puppy version of a

DAILY SCHEDULE

How many relief trips does your puppy need per day? A puppy up to the age of 14 weeks will need to go outside about 8 to 12 times per day! You will have to take the pup out any time he starts sniffing around the floor or turning in small circles, as well as after naps, meals, games and lessons or whenever he's released from his crate. Once the puppy is 14 to 22 weeks of age, he will require only 6 to 8 relief trips. At the ages of 22 to 32 weeks, the puppy will require about 5 to 7 trips. Adult dogs typically require 4 relief trips per day, in the morning, afternoon, evening and before bed.

DON'T BLAME ME

House-training a puppy can be frustrating for the puppy and the owner alike. The puppy does not instinctively understand the difference between defecating on the pavement outside and on the ceramic tile in the kitchen. He is confused and frightened by his human's exuberant reactions to his natural urges. The owner, arguably the more intelligent of the duo, is also frustrated that he cannot convince his puppy to obey his commands and instructions.

In frustration, the owner may struggle with the temptation to discipline the puppy, scold him or even strike him on the rear end. Harsh corrections are unnecessary and inappropriate, serving to defeat your purpose in gaining your puppy's trust and respect. Don't blame your 12-week-old puppy. Blame yourself for not being 100% consistent in the puppy's lessons and routine. The lesson here is simple: try harder and your puppy will succeed.

playpen) within the room of choice is an excellent means of confinement for a young pup, although with an Affenpinscher you must have a secure covering on the pen or else he won't stay confined for long. He can see out and has a certain amount of space in which to run about, but he is safe from dangerous things like electrical cords, heating units, trash baskets or open kitchen-

supply cabinets. Place the pen where the puppy will not get a blast of heat or air conditioning.

In the pen, you can put a few toys, his bed (which can be his crate if the dimensions of pen and crate are compatible) and a few layers of newspaper in one small corner, just in case. A water bowl can be hung at a convenient height on the side of the ex-pen so it won't become a splashing pool for an innovative puppy. Remember, though, what goes in comes out rather quickly, so keep an eye on your pup's water intake during house-training. If it's feeding time, his food dish can go on the floor, next to, but not underneath, the water bowl.

Crates are something that pet owners are at last getting used to for their dogs. Wild or domestic canines have always preferred to sleep in den-like safe spots, and that is exactly what the crate provides. How often have you seen adult dogs that choose to sleep under a table or chair even though they have full run of the house? It's the den connection. If the crate is too large, the Affen will figure out that he can relieve himself in one end and sleep in the other, far away from the mess. Dogs do not want to potty where they sleep.

In your "happy" voice, use the word "Crate" every time you put the pup into his den. If he's new to a crate, toss in a small biscuit for him to chase the first few times. At night, after he's been outside, he should sleep in his crate. The crate may be kept in his designated area at night, or if you want to be sure to hear those wake-up yips in the morning, put the crate in a corner of your bedroom. However, don't make any response whatsoever to whining or crying. If he's completely ignored, he'll settle down and get to sleep.

Good bedding for a young puppy is an old folded bath towel or an old blanket, something that is easily washable and disposable if necessary ("accidents" will happen!). Never put newspaper in the puppy's crate. Also, those old ideas about adding a clock to replace his mother's heartbeat or a hot-water bottle to replace her warmth, are just that—old ideas. The clock could drive the puppy nuts, and the hot-water bottle could end up as a very soggy waterbed. An extremely good breeder would have introduced your puppy to the crate by letting two pups sleep together for a couple of nights, followed by several nights alone. How thankful you will be if you found that breeder!

Safe toys in the pup's crate or area will keep him occupied, but monitor their condition closely. Discard any toys that show signs of being chewed to bits. Squeaky parts, bits of stuffing or plastic or

LEASH TRAINING

House-training and leash training go hand in hand, literally. When taking your puppy outside to do his business, lead him there on his leash. Unless an emergency potty run is called for, do not whisk the puppy up into your arms and take him outside. If you have a fenced yard, you have the advantage of letting the puppy loose to go out, but it's better to put the dog on the leash and take him to his designated place in the yard until he is reliably house-trained. Taking the puppy for a walk is the best way to house-train a dog. The dog will associate the walk with his time to relieve himself, and the exercise of walking stimulates the dog's bowels and bladder. Dogs that are not trained to relieve themselves on a walk may hold it until they get back home, which of course defeats half the purpose of the walk.

any other small pieces can cause intestinal blockage or possibly choking if swallowed.

PROGRESSING WITH POTTY-TRAINING

After you've taken your puppy out and he has relieved himself in the area you've selected, he can have some free time with the family as long as there is someone responsible for watching him. That doesn't mean just someone in the same room who is watching TV or busy on the computer, but rather one person who is doing nothing other than keeping an eye on the pup, play-

"Control" means defining your Affenpinscher's freedom, no matter where you are, for his safety. A wire pen is useful for confining the dog when you are outdoors, as long as there is someone to keep an eye out that he doesn't climb out.

SOGGY HEADLINES

The headlines read: "Puppy Piddles Here!" Breeders commonly use newspapers to line their whelping pens, so puppies learn to associate newspapers with relieving themselves. Do not use newspapers to line your pup's crate, as this will signal to your puppy that it is OK to urinate in his crate. If you choose to paper-train your puppy, you will layer newspapers on a section of the floor near the door he uses to go outside. You should encourage the puppy to use the papers to relieve himself, and bring him there whenever you see him getting ready to go. Little by little, you will reduce the size of the newspaper-covered area so that the puppy will learn to relieve himself "on the other side of the door."

ing with him on the floor and helping him understand his position in the pack.

This first taste of freedom will let you begin to set the house rules. If you don't want the dog on the furniture, now is the time to prevent his first attempts to jump up onto the couch. The word to use in this case is "Off," not "Down." "Down" is the word you will use to teach the down position, which is something entirely different.

Most corrections at this stage come in the form of simply distracting the puppy. Instead of telling him "No" for "Don't chew the carpet," distract the chomping puppy with a toy and he'll forget about the carpet.

As you are playing with the pup, do not forget to watch him closely and pay attention to his body language. Whenever you see him begin to circle or sniff, take the puppy outside to relieve himself. If you are paper-training, put him back into his confined area on the newspapers. In either case, praise him as he eliminates while he actually is *in the act* of relieving himself. Three seconds after he has finished is too late! You'll be praising him for running toward you, picking up a toy or whatever he may be doing at that moment, and that's not what you want to be praising him for. Timing is a vital tool in all dog training. Use it!

SHOULD WE ENROLL?

If you have the means and the time, you should definitely take your dog to obedience classes. Begin with puppy kindergarten classes in which puppies of all sizes learn basic lessons while getting the opportunity to meet and greet each other; it's as much about socialization as it is about good manners. What you learn in class you can practice at home. And if you goof up in practice, you'll get help in the next session.

Remove soiled newspapers immediately and replace them with clean ones. You may want to take a small piece of soiled paper and place it in the middle of the new clean papers, as the scent will attract him to that spot when it's time to go again. That scent attraction is why it's so important to clean up any messes made in the house by using a product specially made to eliminate the odor of dog urine and droppings. Regular household cleansers won't do the trick. Pet

The collar and lead are essential tools for training. The Affenpinscher must be accustomed and comfortable with the collar you select.

shops sell the best pet deodorizers. Invest in the largest container you can find.

Scent attraction eventually will lead your pup to his chosen spot outdoors; this is the basis of outdoor training. When you take your puppy outside to relieve himself, use a one-word command such as "Outside" or "Go-potty" (that's one word to the puppy!) as you attach his leash. Then lead him to his spot. Now comes the hard part—hard for you, that is. Just stand there until he urinates and defecates. Move him a few feet in one direction or another if he's just sitting there looking at you, but remember that this is neither playtime nor time for a walk. This is strictly a business trip! Then, as he circles and squats (remember your timing!), give him a quiet "Good dog" as praise. If you start to jump for joy, ecstatic over his performance, he'll do one of two things: either he will stop mid-stream, as it were, or he'll do it again for you—in the house—and expect you to be just as delighted!

Give him five minutes or so and, if he doesn't go in that time, take him back indoors to his confined area and try again in another ten minutes, or immediately if you see him sniffing and circling. By careful observation, you'll soon work out a successful schedule.

Accidents, by the way, are just that—accidents. Clean them up quickly and thoroughly, without comment, after the puppy has been taken outside to finish his business and then put back into his area or crate. If you witness an accident in progress, say "No!" in a stern voice and get the pup outdoors immediately. No punishment is needed. You and your puppy are just learning each other's language, and sometimes it's easy to miss a puppy's message. Chalk it up to experience and watch more closely from now on.

KEEPING THE PACK ORDERLY
Discipline is a form of training that brings order to life. For exam-

---

"PIDDLE FOR DADDY"

Most dogs love to please their masters; there are no bounds to what dogs will do to make their owners happy. The potty command is a good example of this theory. If toileting on command makes the master happy, then more power to him. Puppies will obligingly piddle if it really makes their keepers smile. Some owners can be creative about which word they will use to command their dogs to relieve themselves. Some popular choices are "Potty," "Tinkle," "Piddle," "Let's go," "Hurry up" and "Toilet." Give the command every time your puppy goes into position and the puppy will begin to associate his business with the command.

ple, military discipline is what allows the soldiers in an army to work as one. Discipline is a form of teaching and, in dogs, is the basis of how the successful pack operates. Each member knows his place in the pack and all respect the leader, or alpha dog. It is essential for your puppy that you establish this type of relationship, with you as the alpha, or leader. It is a form of social coexistence that all canines recognize and accept. Discipline, therefore, is never to be confused with punishment. When you teach your puppy how you want him to behave, and he behaves properly and you praise him for it, you are disciplining him with a form of positive reinforcement.

For a dog, rewards come in the form of praise, a smile, a cheerful tone of voice, a few friendly pats or a rub of the ears. Rewards are also small food treats. Obviously, that does not mean bits of regular dog food. Instead, treats are very small bits of special things like cheese or pieces of soft dog treats. The idea is to reward the dog with something very small that he can taste and swallow, providing instant positive reinforcement. If he has to take time to chew the treat, by the time he is finished he will have forgotten what he did to earn it!

Your puppy should never be physically punished. The displeasure shown on your face

WHO'S TRAINING WHOM?
Dog training is a black-and-white exercise. The correct response to a command must be absolute, and the trainer must insist on completely accurate responses from the dog. A trainer cannot command his dog to sit and then settle for the dog's melting into the down position. Often owners are so pleased that their dogs "did something" in response to a command that they just shrug and say, "OK, down" even though they wanted the dog to sit. You want your dog to respond to the command without hesitation: he must respond at that moment and correctly every time.

and in your voice is sufficient to signal to the pup that he has done something wrong. He wants to please everyone higher up on the social ladder, especially his leader, so a scowl and harsh voice will take care of the error. Growling out the word "Shame!" when the pup is caught in the act of

Your Affenpinscher might view you as his audience rather than as his instructor!

name when you're correcting him. His name is reserved to get his attention for something pleasant about to take place.

There are punishments that have nothing to do with you. For example, your dog may think that chasing cats is one reason for his existence. You can try to stop it as much as you like but without success, because it's such fun for the dog. But one good hissing, spitting swipe of a cat's claws across the dog's nose will put an end to the game forever. Intervene only when your dog's eyeball is seriously at risk. Cat scratches can cause permanent damage to an innocent but annoying puppy.

PUPPY KINDERGARTEN

COLLAR AND LEASH
Before you begin your Affenpinscher puppy's education, he must be used to his collar and leash. Choose a collar for your puppy that is secure, but not heavy or bulky. He won't enjoy training if he's uncomfortable. A flat buckle collar is fine for everyday wear and for initial puppy training. For older dogs, there are several types of training collars such as the head collar, which is similar to a horse's halter. Do not use a chain choke collar with your Affenpinscher. If a training collar is needed, talk to your breeder and a trainer about what's best to use with the breed.

doing something wrong is better than the repetitive "No." Some dogs hear "No" so often that they begin to think it's their name! By the way, do not use the dog's

KEEP SMILING!

While trainers recommend practicing with your dog every day, it's perfectly acceptable to take a "mental health day" off. It's better not to train the dog on days when you're in a sour mood. Your bad attitude or lack of interest will be sensed by your dog, and he will respond accordingly. Studies show that dogs are well tuned in to their humans' emotions. Be conscious of how you use your voice when talking to your dog. Raising your voice or shouting will only erode your dog's trust in you as his trainer and master.

A lightweight 6-foot woven cotton or nylon training leash is preferred by most trainers because it is easy to fold up in your hand and comfortable to hold because there is a certain amount of give to it. There are lessons where the dog will start off 6 feet away from you at the end of the leash. The leash used to take the puppy outside to relieve himself is shorter because you don't want him to roam away from his area. The shorter leash will also be the one to use when you walk the puppy.

If you've been wise enough to enroll in a puppy kindergarten training class, suggestions will be made as to the best collar and leash for your young puppy. I say "wise" because your puppy will be in a class with puppies in his age range (up to five months old) of all breeds and sizes. It's the perfect way for him to learn the right way (and the wrong way) to interact with other dogs as well as their people. You cannot teach your puppy how to interpret another dog's sign language. For a first-time puppy owner, these socialization classes are invaluable. For experienced dog owners, they are a real boon to further training.

Training a bunch of Affens means a bunch of patience! But all must be clear on the rules in order for dogs and owner to live together happily.

ATTENTION
You've been using the dog's name since the minute you collected him from the breeder, so you should be able to get his attention by saying his name—with a big smile and in an excited tone of voice. His response will be the puppy equivalent of "Here I am! What are we going to do?" Your immediate response (if you haven't guessed by now) is "Good dog." Rewarding him at the moment he pays attention to you teaches him the proper way to respond when he hears his name.

The sit exercise is a must for every dog and is a relatively simple lesson to teach.

EXERCISES FOR A BASIC CANINE EDUCATION

THE SIT EXERCISE
There are several ways to teach the puppy to sit. The first one is to catch him whenever he is about to sit and, as his backside nears the floor, say "Sit, good dog!" That's positive reinforcement and, if your timing is sharp, he will learn that what he's doing at that second is connected to your saying "Sit" and that you think he's clever for doing it.

Another method is to start with the puppy on his leash in front of you. Show him a treat in the palm of your right hand. Bring your hand up under his nose and, almost in slow motion, move your hand up and back so his nose goes up in the air and his head tilts back as he follows the treat in your hand. At that point, he will have to either sit or fall over, so as his back legs buckle under, say "Sit, good dog," and then give him the treat and lots of praise.

You may have to begin with your hand lightly running up his chest, actually lifting his chin up until he sits. Some (usually older) dogs require gentle pressure on their hindquarters with the left hand, in which case the dog should be on your left side. Puppies generally do not appreciate this physical dominance.

After a few times, you should be able to show the dog a treat in the open palm of your hand, raise your hand waist-high as you say "Sit" and have him sit. You will thereby have taught him two things at the same time. Both the verbal command and the motion of the hand are signals for the sit. Your puppy is watching you almost more than he is listening to you, so what you do is just as important as what you say.

Don't save any of these drills only for training sessions. Use them as much as possible at odd times during a normal day. The dog should always sit before being given his food dish. He should sit to let you go through a doorway first, when the doorbell rings or when you stop to speak to someone on the street.

If your dog tries to get up from the down position right away, use a hand signal to stop him or guide him back into position.

READY, SIT, GO!

On your marks, get set: train! Most professional trainers agree that the sit command is the place to start your dog's formal education. Sitting is a natural posture for most dogs, and they respond to the sit exercise willingly and readily. For every lesson, begin with the sit command so that you start out with a successful exercise; likewise, you should practice the sit command at the end of every lesson as well because you always want to end on a high note.

THE DOWN EXERCISE

Before beginning to teach the down command, you must consider how the dog feels about this exercise. To him, "down" is a submissive position. Being flat on the floor with you standing over him is not his idea of fun. It's up to you to let him know that, while it may not be fun, the reward of your approval is worth his effort.

Start with the puppy on your left side in a sit position. Hold the leash right above his collar in your left hand. Have an extra-special treat, such as a small piece of cooked chicken or hot dog, in your right hand. Place it at the end of the pup's nose and steadily move your hand down and forward along the ground. Hold the leash to prevent a sudden lunge for the food. As the puppy goes into the down position, say "Down" very gently.

The difficulty with this exercise is twofold: it's both the submissive aspect and the fact that most people say the word "Down" as if they were drill sergeants in charge of recruits! So issue the command sweetly, give him the treat and have the pup

maintain the down position for several seconds. If he tries to get up immediately, place your hands on his shoulders and press down gently, giving him a very quiet "Good dog." As you progress with this lesson, increase the "down time" until he will hold it until you say "Okay" (his cue for release). Practice this one in the house at various times throughout the day.

By increasing the length of time during which the dog must maintain the down position, you'll find many uses for it. For example, he can lie at your feet in the vet's office or anywhere that

Most dogs are quite comfortable lying around to take a break but feel rather differently if commanded to do so.

both of you have to wait, when you are on the phone, while the family is eating and so forth. If you progress to training for competitive obedience, he'll already be all set for the exercise called the "long down."

THE STAY EXERCISE
You can teach your Affenpinscher to stay in the sit, down and stand positions. To teach the sit/stay, have the dog sit on your left side. Hold the leash at waist level in your left hand and let the dog know that you have a treat in your closed right hand. Step forward on your right foot as you say "Stay." Immediately turn and stand directly in front of the dog, keeping your right hand up high so he'll keep his eye on the treat hand and maintain the sit position for a count of five. Return to your original position and offer the reward.

After the basic lessons of sit and down have been mastered, you can progress to teaching your Affenpinscher to stay in either position.

Increase the length of the sit/stay each time until the dog can hold it for at least 30 seconds without moving. After about a week of success, move out on your right foot and take two steps before turning to face the dog. Give the "Stay" hand signal (left palm held up, facing the dog) as you leave. He gets the treat when you return and he holds the sit/stay. Increase the distance that you walk away from him before turning until you reach the length of your training leash. But don't rush it! Go back to the beginning if he moves before he should. No matter what the lesson, never be upset by having to back up for a few days. The repetition and practice are what will make your dog

OKAY!
This is the signal that tells your dog that he can quit whatever he was doing. Use "Okay" to end a session on a correct response to a command. (Never end on an incorrect response.) Lots of praise follows. People use "Okay" a lot and it has other uses for dogs, too. Your dog is barking. You say, "Okay! Come!" "Okay" signals him to stop the barking activity and "Come" allows him to come to you for a "Good dog."

A show dog's knowledge of basic commands is put to the test in the ring, as he must stand and stay for examination by the judge, as well as heel on lead as his gait is evaluated.

reliable in these commands. It won't do any good to move on to something more difficult if the command is not mastered at the easier levels. Above all, even if you do get frustrated, never let your puppy know! Always keep a positive, upbeat attitude during training, which will transmit to your dog for positive results.

The down/stay is taught in the same way once the dog is completely reliable and steady with the down command. Again, don't rush it. With the dog in the down position on your left side, step out on your right foot as you say "Stay." Return by walking around in back of the dog and into your original position. While you are training, it's okay to murmur something like "Hold on" to encourage him to stay put. When the dog will stay without

moving when you are at a distance of 3 or 4 feet, begin to increase the length of time before you return. Be sure he holds the down on your return until you say "Okay." At that point, he gets his treat—just so he'll remember for next time that it's not over until it's over.

THE COME EXERCISE

No command is more important to the safety of your Affenpinscher than "Come." It is what you should say every single time you see the puppy running toward you:

TIPS FOR TRAINING AND SAFETY

1. Whether on or off leash, practice only in a fenced area.
2. Remove the training collar when the training session is over.
3. Don't try to break up a dogfight.
4. "Come," "Leave it" and "Wait" are safety commands.
5. The dog belongs in a crate or behind a barrier when riding in the car.
6. Don't ignore the dog's first sign of aggression. Aggression only gets worse, so take it seriously.
7. Keep the faces of children and dogs separated.
8. Pay attention to what the dog is chewing.
9. Keep the vet's number near your phone.
10. "Okay" is a useful release command.

"Fritzy, come! Good dog." During playtime, run a few feet away from the puppy and turn and tell him to "Come" as he is already running to you. You can go so far as to teach your puppy two things at once if you squat down and hold out your arms. As the pup gets close to you and you're saying "Good dog," bring your right arm in about waist high. Now he's also learning the hand signal, an excellent device should you be on the phone when you need to get him to come to you. You'll also both be one step ahead when you enter obedience classes.

When the puppy responds to your well-timed "Come," try it with the puppy on the training leash. This time, catch him off guard, while he's sniffing a leaf or watching a bird: "Fritzy, come!"

You may have to pause for a split second after his name to be sure you have his attention. If the puppy shows any sign of confusion, give the leash a mild jerk and take a couple of steps backward. Do not repeat the command. In this case, you should say "Good come" as he reaches you.

That's the number-one rule of training. Each command word is given just once. Anything more is nagging. You'll also notice that all commands are one word only. Even when they are actually two words, you say them as one.

Never call the dog to come to you—with or without his name—if you are angry or intend to correct him for some misbehavior. When correcting the pup, you go to him. Your dog must always connect "Come" with something pleasant and with your approval; then you can rely on his response.

Puppies, like children, have notoriously short attention spans, so don't overdo it with any of the training. Keep each lesson short.

You want your Affenpinscher to come running to you this enthusiastically *every* time you call him!

Even with his independent streak and stubborn side, an Affen is quite capable of learning the commands with a patient trainer.

Off-leash heeling is an advanced obedience exercise. Like all off-leash training, it should only be practiced in safely enclosed areas.

Break it up with a quick run around the yard or a ball toss, repeat the lesson and quit as soon as the pup gets it right. That way, you will always end with a "Good dog."

Life isn't perfect and neither are puppies. A time will come, often around ten months of age, when he'll become "selectively deaf" or choose to "forget" his name. He may respond by wagging his tail (and even seeming to smile at you) with a look that says "Make me!" Laugh, throw his favorite toy and skip the lesson you had planned. Pups will be pups!

THE HEEL EXERCISE

The second most important command to teach, after the come, is the heel. When you are walking your growing puppy, you need to be in control. Besides, it looks terrible to have your dog straining at the leash, and it's not much fun

either. At first, your young puppy will probably follow you everywhere, but that's his natural instinct, not your control over the situation. However, any time he does follow you, you can say "Heel" and be ahead of the game, as he will learn to associate this command with the action of following you before you even begin teaching him to heel.

There is a very precise, almost military, procedure for teaching your dog to heel. As with all other obedience training, begin with the dog on your left side. He will be in a very nice sit and you will have the training leash across your chest. Hold the loop and folded leash in your right hand. Pick up the slack leash above the dog in your left hand and hold it loosely at your side. Step out on your left foot as you say "Heel." If the puppy does not move, give a

LET'S GO!

Many people use "Let's go" instead of "Heel" when teaching their dogs to behave on lead. It sounds more like fun! When beginning to teach the heel, whatever command you use, always step off on your left foot. That's the one next to the dog, who is on your left side, in case you've forgotten. Keep a loose leash. When the dog pulls ahead, stop, bring him back and begin again. Use treats to guide him around turns.

gentle tug or pat your left leg to get him started. If he surges ahead of you, stop and pull him back gently until he is at your side. Tell him to sit and begin again.

Walk a few steps and stop while the puppy is correctly beside you. Tell him to sit and give mild verbal praise. (More enthusiastic praise will encourage him to think the lesson is over.) Repeat the lesson, increasing the number of steps you take only as long as the dog is heeling nicely beside you. When you end the lesson, have him hold the sit, then give him the "Okay" to let him know that this is the end of the lesson. Praise him so that he knows he did a good job.

The cure for excessive pulling (a common problem) is to stop when the dog is no more than 2 or 3 feet ahead of you. Guide him back into position and begin again. With a really determined puller, try switching to a head collar. When used correctly, this will automatically turn the pup's head toward you so you can bring him back easily to the heel position. Give quiet, reassuring praise every time the leash goes slack and he's staying with you.

Staying and heeling can take a lot out of a dog, so provide playtime and free-running exercise to shake off the stress when the lessons are over. You don't want him to associate training with all work and no fun.

TIME TO PLAY!

Playtime can happen both indoors and out. A young puppy is growing so rapidly that he needs sleep more than he needs a lot of physical exercise. Puppies get sufficient exercise on their own just through normal puppy activity. Monitor play with young children so you can remove the puppy when he's had enough, or calm the kids if they get too rowdy. Almost all puppies love to chase after a toy you've thrown, and you can turn your games into educational activities. Every time your puppy brings the toy back to you, say "Give it" (or "Drop it") followed by "Good dog" and throwing it again. If he's reluctant to give it to you, offer a small treat so that he drops the toy as he takes the treat. He will soon get the idea.

In this agility exercise which the Affen is practicing, the dog is expected to stop amid the frantic pace of the obstacle course and stay on the platform for a specified length of time.

NO MORE TREATS!

When your dog is responding promptly and correctly to commands, it's time to eliminate treats. Begin by alternating a treat reward with a verbal-praise-only reward. Gradually eliminate all treats while increasing the frequency of praise. Overlook pleading eyes and expectant expressions, but if he's still watching your treat hand, you're on your way to using hand signals.

OBEDIENCE CLASSES

Affenpinscher owners should seriously consider enrolling in obedience classes with their dogs. The experience of working together with your Affen will be rewarding for both of you, and the bond that develops will be even stronger. Achieving success with the Affenpinscher—whether in an obedience class, the competition ring or the show ring—is sweet indeed. If your puppy is intended to be a show dog, show handling classes would be an excellent option as well. Many areas have dog clubs that offer basic obedience training as well as preparatory classes for obedience competition. There are also local dog trainers who offer similar classes.

Although Affens are rarely seen competing at obedience shows, nothing is impossible with dedication and training. Despite the breed's stubbornness and independence, the Affenpinscher is a highly intelligent dog that can earn titles at various levels of

Approaching an agility jump. For small dogs like the Affenpinscher, agility obstacles are lowered in height accordingly.

competition. The beginning levels of obedience competition, including basic behaviors such as sit, down, heel, etc., are certainly within the reach of the well-trained Affenpinscher.

TRAINING FOR OTHER ACTIVITIES

Once your dog has basic obedience under his collar and is 12 months of age, you can enter the world of agility training. Dogs think agility is pure fun, like being turned loose in an amusement park full of obstacles! Agility is fast-paced and exciting, with dog and handler working together to negotiate the course. Tracking tests a dog's scenting ability and is open to all "nosey" dogs (which would include all dogs!). For those who like to volunteer, there is the wonderful feeling of owning a therapy dog and visiting hospices, nursing homes and veterans' homes to bring smiles, comfort and companionship to those who live there.

Around the house, your Affenpinscher can be taught to do some simple chores. You might teach him to carry or fetch small household items. The kids can teach the dog all kinds of tricks, from playing hide-and-seek to rolling over and more. A family dog is what rounds out the family. Everything he does, including sitting on your lap and gazing lovingly at you, represents the bonus of owning a dog.

Can you believe the agility and intelligence packed into such a small dog? This Affenpinscher is practicing for an agility competition.

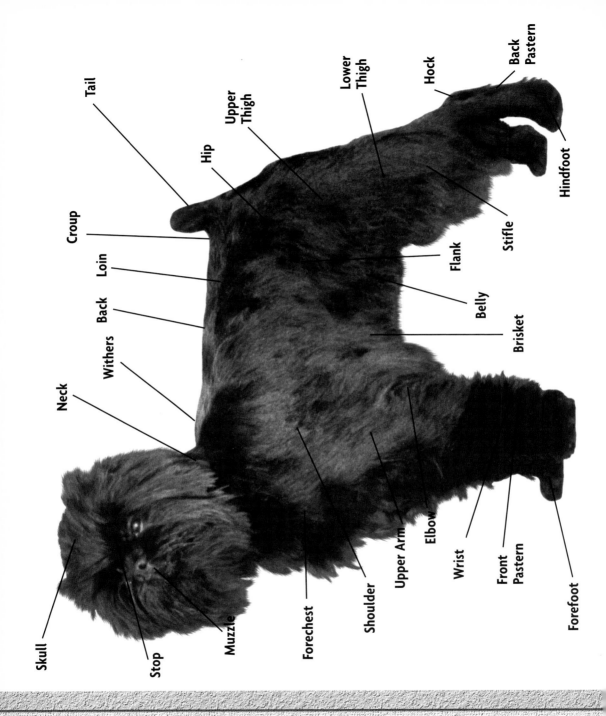

Tail

Back
Pastern

Lower
Thigh

Hock

Upper
Thigh

Hindfoot

Hip

Croup

Stifle

Loin

Flank

Back

Belly

Withers

Brisket

Neck

Skull

Stop

Muzzle

Forechest

Shoulder

Upper Arm

Elbow

Wrist

Front
Pastern

Forefoot

PHYSICAL STRUCTURE OF THE AFFENPINSCHER

AFFENPINSCHER

By Lowell Ackerman DVM, DACVD

HEALTHCARE FOR A LIFETIME

When you own a dog, you become his healthcare advocate over his entire lifespan, as well as being the one to shoulder the financial burden of such care. Accordingly, it is worthwhile to focus on prevention rather than treatment, as you and your pet will both be happier.

Of course, the best place to have begun your program of preventive healthcare is with the initial purchase or adoption of your dog. There is no way of guaranteeing that your new furry friend is free of medical problems, but there are some things you can do to improve your odds. You certainly should have done adequate research into the Affenpinscher and have selected your puppy carefully rather than buying on impulse. Health issues aside, a large number of pet abandonment and relinquishment cases arise from a mismatch between pet needs and owner expectations. This is entirely preventable with appropriate planning and finding a good breeder.

Regarding healthcare issues specifically, it is very difficult to make blanket statements about where to acquire a problem-free

> ### TAKING YOUR DOG'S TEMPERATURE
>
> It is important to know how to take your dog's temperature at times when you think he may be ill. It's not the most enjoyable task, but it can be done without too much difficulty. It's easier with a helper, preferably someone with whom the dog is friendly, so that one of you can hold the dog while the other inserts the thermometer.
>
> Before inserting the thermometer, coat the end with petroleum jelly. Insert the thermometer slowly and gently into the dog's rectum about one inch. Wait for the reading, about two minutes. Be sure to remove the thermometer carefully and clean it thoroughly after each use.
>
> A dog's normal body temperature is between 100.5 and 102.5 degrees F. Immediate veterinary attention is required if the dog's temperature is below 99 or above 104 degrees F.

1. Esophagus
2. Lungs
3. Gall Bladder
4. Liver
5. Stomach
6. Intestines
7. Urinary Bladder

INTERNAL ORGANS OF THE AFFENPINSCHER

pet, but, again, a reputable breeder is your best bet. In an ideal situation you have the opportunity to see both parents, get references from other owners of the breeder's pups and see genetic-testing documentation for several generations of the litter's ancestors. At the very least, you must thoroughly investigate the Affenpinscher and the problems inherent in that breed, as well as the genetic testing available to screen for those problems. Genetic testing offers some important benefits, but testing is available for only a few disorders in a relatively small number of breeds and is not available for some of the most common genetic diseases, such as hip dysplasia, cataracts, epilepsy, cardiomyopathy, etc. This area of research is indeed exciting and increasingly important, and advances will continue

to be made each year. In fact, recent research has shown that there is an equivalent dog gene for 75% of known human genes, so research done in either species is likely to benefit the other.

We've also discussed that evaluating the behavioral nature of your Affenpinscher and that of his immediate family members is an important part of the selection process that cannot be underestimated or overemphasized. It is sometimes difficult to evaluate temperament in puppies because certain behavioral tendencies, such as some forms of aggression, may not be immediately evident. More dogs are euthanized each year for behavioral reasons than for all medical conditions combined, so it is critical to take temperament issues seriously. Start with a well-balanced, friendly companion and put the time and effort into proper socialization, and you will both be rewarded with a valued relationship for the life of the dog.

Assuming that you have started off with a pup from healthy, sound stock, you then become responsible for helping your veterinarian keep your pet healthy. Some crucial things happen before you even bring your puppy home. Parasite control typically begins at two weeks of age, and vaccinations typically begin at six to eight weeks of age. A pre-pubertal

WARNING SIGNS

A veterinary dental exam is necessary if you notice one or any combination of the following in your dog:
- Broken, loose or missing teeth
- Loss of appetite (which could be due to mouth pain or illness caused by infection)
- Gum abnormalities, including redness, swelling and bleeding
- Drooling, with or without blood
- Yellowing of the teeth or gumline, indicating tartar
- Bad breath

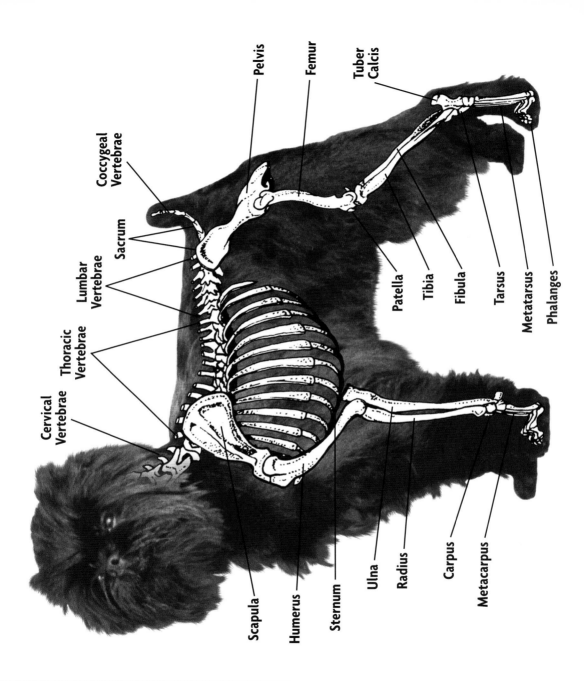

Pelvis

Femur

Tuber Calcis

Coccygeal Vertebrae

Sacrum

Lumbar Vertebrae

Thoracic Vertebrae

Cervical Vertebrae

Patella

Tibia

Fibula

Tarsus

Metatarsus

Phalanges

Scapula

Humerus

Sternum

Ulna

Radius

Carpus

Metacarpus

SKELETAL STRUCTURE OF THE AFFENPINSCHER

evaluation is typically scheduled for about six months of age. At this time, a dental evaluation is done (since the adult teeth are now in), heartworm prevention is started and neutering or spaying is most commonly done.

It is critical to commence regular dental care at home if you have not already done so. It may not sound very important, but most dogs have active periodontal disease by four years of age if they don't have their teeth cleaned regularly at home, not just at their veterinary exams. Dental problems lead to more than just bad "doggy breath." Gum disease can have very serious medical consequences. If you start brushing your dog's teeth and using antiseptic rinses from a young age, your dog will be accustomed to it and will not resist. The results will be healthy dentition, which your pet will need to enjoy a long, healthy life.

Most dogs are considered adults at a year of age, although the Affenpinscher will still have some filling out to do up to about two or three years old. Even individual dogs within each breed have different health-care requirements, so work with your veterinarian to determine what will be needed and what your role should be. This doctor-client relationship is important

Healthy and fit in her senior years, here's Kyleakin Maid At Yarrow.

**YOUR DOG NEEDS
TO VISIT THE VET IF:**

- He has ingested a toxin such as antifreeze or a toxic plant; in these cases, administer first aid and call the vet right away
- His teeth are discolored, loose or missing or he has sores or other signs of infection or abnormality in the mouth
- He has been vomiting, has had diarrhea or has been constipated for over 24 hours; call immediately if you notice blood
- He has refused food for over 24 hours
- His eating habits, water intake or toilet habits have noticeably changed; if you have noticed weight gain or weight loss
- He shows symptoms of bloat, which requires *immediate* attention
- He is salivating excessively
- He has a lump in his throat
- He has a lump or bumps anywhere on the body
- He is very lethargic
- He appears to be in pain or otherwise has trouble chewing or swallowing
- His skin loses elasticity
  Of course, there will be other instances in which a visit to the vet is necessary; these are just some of the signs that could be indicative of serious problems that need to be caught as early as possible.

because as vaccination guidelines change there may not be an annual "vaccine visit" scheduled. You must make sure that you see your veterinarian at least annually, even if no vaccines are due, because this is the best opportunity to coordinate healthcare activities and to make sure that no medical issues creep by unaddressed.

When your Affenpinscher reaches three-quarters of his anticipated lifespan, he is considered a "senior" and likely requires some special care. In general, if you've been taking great care of your canine companion throughout his formative and adult years, the transition to senior status should be a smooth one. Age is not a disease, and as long as everything is functioning as it should, there is no reason why most of late adulthood should not be rewarding for both you and your pet. This is especially true if you have tended to the details, such as regular veterinary visits, proper dental care, excellent nutrition and management of bone and joint issues.

At this stage in your Affenpinscher's life, your veterinarian should want to schedule visits twice yearly, instead of once, to run some laboratory screenings, electrocardiograms and the like, and to change the diet to something more digestible. Catching problems early is the best way to manage them effectively. Treating the early stages of heart disease is so much easier than trying to intervene when there is more significant damage to the heart muscle. Similarly, managing the beginning of kidney problems is fairly routine if there is no significant kidney damage. Other problems, like cognitive dysfunction (similar to senility and Alzheimer's disease), cancer, diabetes and arthritis, are more common in older dogs, but all can be treated to help the dog live as many happy, comfortable years as possible. Just as in people, medical management is more effective (and less expensive) when you catch things early.

SELECTING A VETERINARIAN
There is probably no more important decision that you will make regarding your pet's healthcare than the selection of his doctor. Your pet's veterinarian will be a pediatrician, family-practice physician and gerontologist, depending on the dog's life stage, and will be the individual who makes recommendations regarding issues such as when specialists need to be consulted, when diagnostic testing and/or therapeutic intervention is needed and when you will need to seek outside emergency and critical-care services. Your vet will act as your advocate and liaison throughout these processes.

PROBLEM: AND THAT STARTS WITH "P"
Urinary tract problems more commonly affect female dogs, especially those who have been spayed. The first sign that a urinary tract problem exists usually is a strong odor from the urine or an unusual color. Blood in the urine, known as hematuria, is another sign of an infection, related to cystitis, a bladder infection, bladder cancer or a blood-clotting disorder. Urinary tract problems can also be signaled by the dog's straining while urinating, experiencing pain during urination and genital discharge as well as excessive water intake and urination.

Excessive drinking, in and of itself, does not indicate a urinary tract problem. A dog who is drinking more than normal may have a kidney or liver problem, a hormonal disorder or diabetes mellitus. Behaviorists report a disorder known as psychogenic polydipsia, which manifests itself in excessive drinking and urination. If you notice your dog drinking much more than normal, take him to the vet.

Everyone has his own idea about what to look for in a vet, an individual who will play a big role in his dog's (and, of course, his own) life for many years to come. For some, it is the compassionate caregiver with whom they hope to develop a professional relationship to span the lifetime of their dogs and even their future pets. For others, they are seeking a clinician with keen diagnostic and therapeutic insight who can deliver state-of-the-art healthcare. Still others need a veterinary facility that is open evenings and weekends, is in close proximity or provides mobile veterinary services to accommodate their schedules; these people may not much mind that their dogs might see different veterinarians on each visit. Just as we have different reasons for selecting our own healthcare professionals (e.g., covered by insurance plan, expert in field, convenient location, etc.), we should not expect that there is a one-size-fits-all recommendation for selecting a veterinarian and veterinary practice. The best advice is to be honest in your assessment of what you expect from a veterinary practice and to conscientiously research the options in your area. You will quickly appreciate that not all veterinary practices are the same, and you will be happiest with one that truly meets your needs.

There is another point to be considered in the selection of veterinary services. Not that long ago, a single veterinarian would attempt to manage all medical and surgical issues as they arose. That was often problematic because veterinarians are trained in many species and many diseases, and it

was just impossible for general veterinary practitioners to be experts in every species, every breed, every field and every ailment. However, just as in the human healthcare fields, specialization has allowed general practitioners to concentrate on primary healthcare delivery, especially wellness and the prevention of infectious diseases, and to utilize a network of specialists to assist in the management of conditions that require specific expertise and experience. Thus there are now many types of veterinary specialists, including dermatologists, cardiologists, ophthalmologists, surgeons, internists, oncologists, neurologists, behaviorists, criticalists and others to help primary-care veterinarians deal with complicated medical challenges. In most cases, specialists see cases referred by primary-care veterinarians, make diagnoses and set up management plans. From there, the animals' ongoing care is returned to their primary-care veterinarians. This important team approach to your pet's medical-care needs has provided opportunities for advanced care and an unparalleled level of quality to be delivered.

With all of the opportunities for your Affenpinscher to receive high-quality veterinary medical care, there is another topic that needs to be addressed at the same time—cost. It's been said that you

A beautiful Affenpinsher and top winner, this is Ch. Tamarin Tip-Off, bred by Jacqueline L. Stacy and owned by Dr. Loren G. Lipson.

COMMON INFECTIOUS DISEASES

Let's discuss some of the diseases that create the need for vaccination in the first place. Following are the major canine infectious diseases and a simple explanation of each.

Rabies: A devastating viral disease that can be fatal in dogs and people. In fact, vaccination of dogs and cats is an important public-health measure to create a resistant animal buffer population to protect people from contracting the disease. Vaccination schedules are determined on a government level and are not optional for pet owners; rabies vaccination is required by law in all 50 states.

Parvovirus: A severe, potentially life-threatening disease that is easily transmitted between dogs. There are four strains of the virus, but it is believed that there is significant "cross-protection" between strains that may be included in individual vaccines.

Distemper: A potentially severe and life-threatening disease with a relatively high risk of exposure, especially in certain regions. In very high-risk distemper environments, young pups may be vaccinated with human measles vaccine, a related virus that offers cross-protection when administered at four to ten weeks of age.

Hepatitis: Caused by canine adenovirus type 1 (CAV-1), but since vaccination with the causative virus has a higher rate of adverse effects, cross-protection is derived from the use of adenovirus type 2 (CAV-2), a cause of respiratory disease and one of the potential causes of canine cough. Vaccination with CAV-2 provides long-term immunity against hepatitis, but relatively less protection against respiratory infection.

Canine cough: Also called tracheobronchitis, actually a fairly complicated result of viral and bacterial offenders; therefore, even with vaccination, protection is incomplete. Wherever dogs congregate, canine cough will likely be spread among them. Intranasal vaccination with *Bordetella* and parainfluenza is the best safeguard, but the duration of immunity does not appear to be very long, typically a year at most. These are non-core vaccines, but vaccination is sometimes mandated by boarding kennels, obedience classes, dog shows and other places where dogs congregate to try to minimize spread of infection.

Leptospirosis: A potentially fatal disease that is more common in some geographic regions. It is capable of being spread to humans. The disease varies with the individual "serovar," or strain, of *Leptospira* involved. Since there does not appear to be much cross-protection between serovars, protection is only as good as the likelihood that the serovar in the vaccine is the same as the one in the pet's local environment. Problems with *Leptospira* vaccines are that protection does not last very long, side effects are not uncommon and a large percentage of dogs (perhaps 30%) may not respond to vaccination.

Borrelia burgdorferi: The cause of Lyme disease, the risk of which varies with the geographic area in which the pet lives and travels. Lyme disease is spread by deer ticks in the eastern US and western black-legged ticks in the western part of the country, and the risk of exposure is high in some regions. Lameness, fever and inappetence are most commonly seen in affected dogs. The extent of protection from the vaccine has not been conclusively demonstrated.

Coronavirus: This disease has a high risk of exposure, especially in areas where dogs congregate, but it typically causes only mild to moderate digestive upset (diarrhea, vomiting, etc.). Vaccines are available, but the duration of protection is believed to be relatively short and the effectiveness of the vaccine in preventing infection is considered low.

There are many other vaccinations available, including those for *Giardia* and canine adenovirus-1. While there may be some specific indications for their use, and local risk factors to be considered, they are not widely recommended for most dogs.

can have excellent healthcare or inexpensive healthcare, but never both; this is as true in veterinary medicine as it is in human medicine. While veterinary costs are a fraction of what the same services cost in the human healthcare arena, it is still difficult to deal with unanticipated medical costs, especially since they can easily creep into hundreds or even thousands of dollars if specialists or emergency services become involved. However, there are ways of managing these risks. The easiest is to buy pet health insurance and realize that its foremost purpose is not to cover routine healthcare visits but rather to serve as an umbrella for those rainy days when your pet needs medical care and you don't want to worry about whether or not you can afford that care.

Pet insurance policies are very cost-effective (and very inexpensive by human health-insurance standards), but make sure that you buy the policy long before you intend to use it (preferably starting in puppyhood, because coverage will exclude pre-existing conditions) and that you are actually buying an indemnity insurance plan from an insurance company that is regulated by your state or province. Many insurance policy look-alikes are actually discount clubs that are redeemable only at specific locations and for specific services. An indemnity plan

covers your pet at almost all veterinary, specialty and emergency practices and is an excellent way to manage your pet's ongoing healthcare needs.

VACCINATIONS AND INFECTIOUS DISEASES

There has never been an easier time to prevent a variety of infectious diseases in your dog, but the advances we've made in veterinary medicine come with a price—choice. Now while it may seem that choice is a good thing (and it is), it has never been more difficult for the pet owner (or the veterinarian) to make an informed decision about the best way to protect pets through vaccination.

Years ago, it was just accepted that puppies got a starter series of vaccinations and then annual "boosters" throughout their lives to keep them protected. As more and more vaccines became available, consumers wanted the convenience of having all of that protection in a single injection. The result was "multivalent" vaccines that crammed a lot of protection into a single syringe. The manufacturers' recommendations were to give the vaccines annually, and this was a simple enough protocol to follow. However, as veterinary medicine has become more sophisticated and we have started looking more at healthcare quandaries rather than convenience, it became necessary to reevaluate the situation and deal with some tough questions. It is important to realize that whether or not to use a particular vaccine depends on the risk of contracting the disease against which it protects, the severity of the disease if it is contracted, the duration of immunity provided by the vaccine, the safety of the product and the needs of the individual animal. In a very general sense, rabies, distemper, hepatitis and parvovirus are considered core vaccine needs, while parainfluenza, *Bordetella bronchiseptica*, leptospirosis, coronavirus and borreliosis (Lyme disease) are considered non-core needs and best reserved for animals that demonstrate reasonable risk of contracting the diseases.

THE GREAT VACCINATION DEBATE

What kinds of questions need to be addressed? When the vet injects multiple organisms at the same time, might some of the components interfere with one another in the development of immunologic protection? We don't have the comprehensive answer for that question, but it does appear that the immune system better handles agents when given individually. Unfortunately, most manufacturers still bundle their vaccine components because that is what most pet owners want, so getting vaccines with single components can sometimes be difficult.

Another question has to do with how often vaccines should be given. Again, this seems to be different for each vaccine component. There seems to be a general consensus that a puppy (or a dog with an unknown vaccination history) should get a series of vaccinations to initially stimulate his immunity and then a booster at one year of age, but even the veterinary associations and colleges have trouble reaching agreement about what he should get after that. Rabies vaccination schedules are not debated because vaccine schedules for this contagious and devastating disease are determined by government agencies. Regarding the rest, some recommend that we continue to give the vaccines annually because this method has worked well as a disease preventive for decades and delivers predictable protection. Others recommend that some of the vaccines need to be given only every second or third year, as this can be done without affecting levels of protection. This is probably true for some vaccine components (such as hepatitis), but there have been no large studies to demonstrate what the optimal interval should be and whether the same principles hold true for all breeds.

It may be best to just measure titers, which are protective blood levels of various vaccine components, on an annual basis, but that too is not without controversy. Scientists have not precisely determined the minimum titer of specific vaccine components that will be guaranteed to provide a pet with protection. Pets with very high titers will clearly be protected and those with very low titers will need repeat vaccinations, but there is also a large "gray zone" of pets that probably have intermediate protection and may or may not need repeat vaccination, depending on their risk of coming into contact with the disease.

These questions leave primary-care veterinarians in a very uncomfortable position, one that is not easy to resolve. Do they recommend annual vaccination in a manner that has demonstrated successful protection for decades, do they recommend skipping vaccines some years and hope that the protection lasts or do they measure blood tests (titers) and hope that the results are convincing enough to clearly indicate whether repeat vaccination is warranted?

These aren't the only vaccination questions impacting pets, owners and veterinarians. Other controversies focus on whether vaccines should be dosed accord-

One of today's top-winning Affenpinschers, Ch. Hilane's Just Look At Me, owned by Sandra Lex, is the picture of good health and fitness.

ing to body weight (currently they are administered in uniform doses, regardless of the animal's size), whether there are breed-specific issues important in determining vaccination programs (for instance, we know that some breeds have a harder time mounting an appropriate immune response to parvovirus vaccine and might benefit from a different dose or injection interval) and which type of vaccine—live-virus or inactivated—offers more advantages with fewer disadvantages. Clearly, there are many more questions than there are answers. The important thing, as a pet owner, is to be aware of the issues and be able to work with your veterinarian to make decisions that are right for your pet.

NEUTERING/SPAYING
Sterilization procedures (neutering for males/spaying for females) are meant to accomplish several purposes. While the underlying premise is to address the risk of pet overpopulation, there are some medical and behavioral benefits to the surgeries as well. For females, spaying prior to the first estrus (heat cycle) leads to a marked reduction in the risk of mammary cancer. There also will be no manifestations of "heat" to attract male dogs and no bleeding in the house. For males, there is prevention of testicular cancer and a reduction in the risk of prostate problems. In both sexes there may be some limited reduction in aggressive behaviors toward other dogs, and some diminishing of urine marking, roaming and mounting.

While neutering and spaying do indeed prevent animals from contributing to pet overpopulation, even no-cost and low-cost neutering options have not eliminated the problem. Perhaps one of the main reasons for this is that individuals that intentionally breed their dogs and those that allow their animals to run at large are the main causes of

unwanted offspring. Also, animals in shelters are often there because they were abandoned or relinquished, not because they came from unplanned matings. Neutering/spaying is important, but it should be considered in the context of the real causes of animals' ending up in shelters and eventually being euthanized.

One of the important considerations regarding neutering is that it is a surgical procedure.

SPAY'S THE WAY
Although spaying a female dog qualifies as major surgery—an ovariohysterectomy, in fact—this procedure is regarded as routine when performed by a qualified veterinarian on a healthy dog. The advantages to spaying a bitch are many and great. Spayed dogs do not develop uterine cancer or any life-threatening diseases of the genitals. Likewise, spayed dogs are at a significantly reduced risk of breast cancer. Bitches (and owners) are relieved of the demands of heat cycles. A spayed bitch will not leave bloody stains on your furniture during estrus, and you will not have to contend with single-minded macho males trying to climb your fence in order to seduce her. The spayed bitch's coat will not show the ill effects of her estrogen level's climbing such as a dull, lackluster outer coat or patches of hairlessness.

This sometimes gets lost in discussions of low-cost procedures and commoditization of the process. In females, spaying is specifically referred to as an ovariohysterectomy. In this procedure, a midline incision is made in the abdomen and the entire uterus and both ovaries are surgically removed. While this is a major invasive surgical procedure, it usually has few complications because it is typically performed on healthy young animals. However, it is major surgery, as any woman who has had a hysterectomy will attest.

In males, neutering has traditionally referred to castration, which involves the surgical removal of both testicles. While still a significant piece of surgery, there is not the abdominal exposure that is required in the female surgery. In addition, there is now a chemical sterilization option, in which a solution is injected into each testicle, leading to atrophy of the sperm-producing cells. This can typically be done under sedation rather than full anesthesia. This is a relatively new approach, and there are no long-term clinical studies yet available.

Neutering/spaying is typically done around six months of age at most veterinary hospitals, although techniques have been pioneered to perform the proce-

dures in animals as young as eight weeks of age. In general, the surgeries on the very young animals are done for the specific reason of sterilizing them before they go to their new homes. This is done in some shelter hospitals for assurance that the animals will definitely not produce any pups. Otherwise, these organizations need to rely on owners to comply with their wishes to have the animals "altered" at a later date, something that does not always happen.

Most breeders will recommend that you spay/neuter your pet dogs. Unless you are showing and breeding your Affenpinscher, this is sound advice. Here are two favorite show winners, Magilla and Belle, owned by the Clapps.

A scanning electron micrograph of a dog flea, Ctenocephalides canis, on dog hair

EXTERNAL PARASITES

FLEAS

Fleas have been around for millions of years and, while we have better tools now for controlling them than at any time in the past, there still is little chance that they will end up on an endangered species list. Actually, they are very well adapted to living on our pets, and they continue to adapt as we make advances.

The female flea can consume 15 times her weight in blood during active reproduction and can lay as many as 40 eggs a day. These eggs are very resistant to the effects of insecticides. They hatch into larvae, which then mature and spin cocoons. The immature fleas reside in this pupal stage until the time is right for feeding. This pupal stage is also very resistant to the effects of insecticides, and pupae can last in the environment without feeding for many months. Newly emergent fleas are attracted to animals by the warmth of the animals' bodies, movement and exhaled carbon dioxide. However, when they first emerge from their cocoons, they orient towards light; thus when an animal passes between a flea and the light source, casting a shadow, the flea pounces and starts to feed. If the animal turns out to be a dog or cat, the reproductive cycle continues. If the flea lands on another type of animal, including a person, the flea will bite but will then look for a more appropriate host. An emerging adult flea can survive without feeding for up to 12 months but, once it tastes blood, it can survive off its host for only 3 to 4 days.

It was once thought that fleas spend most of their lives in the environment, but we now know that fleas won't willingly jump off a dog unless leaping to another dog or when physically removed by brushing, bathing or other manipulation. Flea eggs, on the other hand, are shiny and smooth, and they roll off the animal and into the environment. The eggs, larvae and pupae then exist in the environment, but once the adult finds a susceptible animal, it's home sweet home until the flea is forced to seek refuge elsewhere.

Since adult fleas live on the animal and immature forms survive in the environment, a successful treatment plan must address all stages of the flea life cycle. There are now several safe and effective flea-control products that can be applied on a monthly

> ### FLEA PREVENTION FOR YOUR DOG
> - Discuss with your veterinarian the safest product to protect your dog, likely in the form of a monthly tablet or a liquid preparation placed on the back of the dog's neck.
> - For dogs suffering from flea-bite dermatitis, a shampoo or topical insecticide treatment is required.
> - Your lawn and property should be sprayed with an insecticide designed to kill fleas and ticks that lurk outdoors.
> - Using a flea comb, check the dog's coat regularly for any signs of parasites.
> - Practice good housekeeping. Vacuum floors, carpets and furniture regularly, especially in the areas that the dog frequents, and wash the dog's bedding weekly.
> - Follow up house-cleaning with carpet shampoos and sprays to rid the house of fleas at all stages of development. Insect growth regulators are the safest option.

basis. These include fipronil, imidacloprid, selamectin and permethrin (found in several formulations). Most of these products have significant flea-killing rates within 24 hours. However, none of them will control the immature forms in the environment. To accomplish this, there are a variety of insect growth regulators that can be sprayed into

THE FLEA'S LIFE CYCLE

What came first, the flea or the egg? This age-old mystery is more difficult to comprehend than the actual cycle of the flea. Fleas usually live only about four months. A female can lay 2,000 eggs in her lifetime.

Egg

After ten days of rolling around your carpet or under your furniture, the eggs hatch into larvae, which feed on various and sundry debris. In days or months, depending on the climate, the larvae spin cocoons and develop into the pupal or nymph stage, which quickly develop into fleas.

Larva

Pupa

These immature fleas must locate a host within 10 to 14 days or they will die. Only about 1% of the flea population exist as adult fleas, while the other 99% exist as eggs, larvae or pupae.

KILL FLEAS THE NATURAL WAY

If you choose not to go the route of conventional medication, there are some natural ways to ward off fleas:

- Dust your dog with a natural flea powder, composed of such herbal goodies as rosemary, wormwood, pennyroyal, citronella, rue, tobacco powder and eucalyptus.
- Apply diatomaceous earth, the fossilized remains of single-cell algae, to your carpets, furniture and pet's bedding. Even though it's not good for dogs, it's even worse for fleas, which will dry up swiftly and die.
- Brush your dog frequently, give him adequate exercise and let him fast occasionally. All of these activities strengthen the dog's immune system and make him more resistant to disease and parasites.
- Bathe your dog with a capful of pennyroyal or eucalyptus oil.
- Feed a natural diet, free of additives and preservatives. Add some fresh garlic and brewer's yeast to the dog's morning portion, as these items have flea-repelling properties.

the environment (e.g., pyriproxyfen, methoprene, fenoxycarb) as well as insect development inhibitors such as lufenuron that can be administered. These compounds have no effect on adult fleas, but they stop immature forms from developing into adults. In years gone by, we relied heavily on toxic insecticides (such as organophosphates, organochlorines and carbamates) to manage the flea problem, but today's options are not only much safer to use on our pets but also safer for the environment.

TICKS

Ticks are members of the spider class (arachnids) and are blood-sucking parasites capable of transmitting a variety of diseases, including Lyme disease, ehrlichiosis, babesiosis and Rocky Mountain spotted fever. It's easy to see ticks on your own skin, but it is more of a challenge when your furry companion is affected. Whenever you happen to be planning a stroll in a tick-infested area (especially forests, grassy or wooded areas or parks) be prepared to do a thorough inspection of your dog afterward to search for ticks. Ticks can be tricky, so make sure you spend time looking in the ears, between the toes and everywhere else where a tick might hide. Ticks need to be attached for 24–72 hours before they transmit most of the diseases that they carry, so you do have a window of opportunity for some preventive intervention.

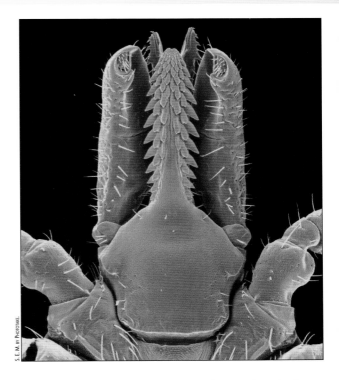

S. E. M. BY PHOTOTAKE.

A scanning electron micrograph of the head of a female deer tick, *Ixodes dammini,* a parasitic tick that carries Lyme disease.

A TICKING BOMB

There is nothing good about a tick's harpooning his nose into your dog's skin. Among the diseases caused by ticks are Rocky Mountain spotted fever, canine ehrlichiosis, canine babesiosis, canine hepatozoonosis and Lyme disease. If a dog is allergic to the saliva of a female wood tick, he can develop tick paralysis.

Female ticks live to eat and breed. They can lay between 4,000 and 5,000 eggs and they die soon after. Males, on the other hand, live only to mate with the females and continue the process as long as they are able. Most ticks live on multiple hosts before parasitizing dogs. The immature forms typically reside on grass and shrubs, waiting for susceptible animals to walk by. The larvae and nymph stages typically feed on wildlife.

If only a few ticks are present on a dog, they can be plucked out, but it is important to remove the entire head and mouthparts,

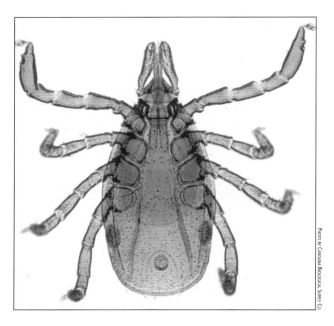

Photo by Carolina Biological Supply Co.

Deer tick,
Ixodes dammini.

of in a container of alcohol or household bleach.

Some of the newer flea products, specifically those with fipronil, selamectin and permethrin, have effect against some, but not all, species of tick. Flea collars containing appropriate pesticides (e.g., propoxur, chlorfenvinphos) can aid in tick control. In most areas, such collars should be placed on animals in March, at the beginning of the tick season, and changed regularly. Leaving the collar on when the pesticide level is waning invites the development of resistance. Amitraz collars are also good for tick control, and the active ingredient does not interfere with other flea-control products. The ingredient helps prevent the attachment of ticks to the skin and will cause those ticks already on the skin to detach themselves.

which may be deeply embedded in the skin. This is best accomplished with forceps designed especially for this purpose; fingers can be used but should be protected with rubber gloves, plastic wrap or at least a paper towel. The tick should be grasped as closely as possible to the animal's skin and should be pulled upward with steady, even pressure. Do not squeeze, crush or puncture the body of the tick or you risk exposure to any disease carried by that tick. Once the ticks have been removed, the sites of attachment should be disinfected. Your hands should then be washed with soap and water to further minimize risk of contagion. The tick should be disposed

TICK CONTROL

Removal of underbrush and leaf litter and the thinning of trees in areas where tick control is desired are recommended. These actions remove the cover and food sources for small animals that serve as hosts for ticks. With continued mowing of grasses in these areas, the probability of ticks' surviving is further reduced. A variety of insecticide ingredients (e.g., resmethrin, carbaryl, permethrin, chlorpyrifos, dioxathion and allethrin) are registered for tick control around the home.

MITES

Mites are tiny arachnid parasites that parasitize the skin of dogs. Skin diseases caused by mites are referred to as "mange," and there are many different forms seen in dogs. These forms are very different from one another, each one warranting an individual description.

Sarcoptic mange, or scabies, is one of the itchiest conditions that affects dogs. The microscopic *Sarcoptes* mites burrow into the superficial layers of the skin and can drive dogs crazy with itchiness. They are also communicable to people, although they can't complete their reproductive cycle on people. In addition to being tiny, the mites also are often difficult to find when trying to make a diagnosis. Skin scrapings from multiple areas are examined microscopically but, even then, sometimes the mites cannot be found.

Fortunately, scabies is relatively easy to treat, and there are a variety of products that will successfully kill the mites. Since the mites can't live in the environment for very long without feeding, a complete cure is usually possible within four to eight weeks.

Cheyletiellosis is caused by a relatively large mite, which sometimes can be seen even without a microscope. Often referred to as "walking dandruff," this also causes itching, but not usually as profound as with scabies. While *Cheyletiella* mites can survive somewhat longer

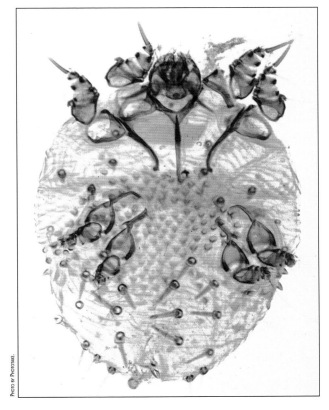

PHOTO BY PHOTOTAKE.

Sarcoptes scabiei, commonly known as the "itch mite."

in the environment than scabies mites, they too are relatively easy to treat, being responsive to not only the medications used to treat scabies but also often to flea-control products.

Otodectes cynotis is the canine ear mite and is one of the more common causes of mange, especially in young dogs in shelters or pet stores. That's because the mites are typically present in large numbers and are quickly spread to nearby animals. The mites rarely do much harm but can be difficult

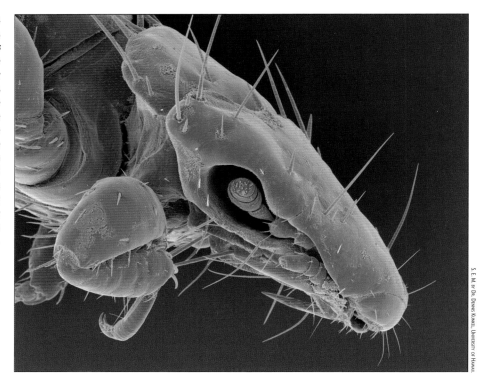

Micrograph of a dog louse, *Heterodoxus spiniger.* Female lice attach their eggs to the hairs of the dog. As the eggs hatch, the larval lice bite and feed on the blood. Lice can also feed on dead skin and hair. This feeding activity can cause hair loss and skin problems.

S. E. M. BY DR. DENNIS KUNKEL, UNIVERSITY OF HAWAII.

to eradicate if the treatment regimen is not comprehensive. While many try to treat the condition with ear drops only, this is the most common cause of treatment failure. Ear drops cause the mites to simply move out of the ears and as far away as possible (usually to the base of the tail) until the insecticide levels in the ears drop to an acceptable level—then it's back to business as usual! The successful treatment of ear mites requires treating all animals in the household with a systemic insecticide, such as selamectin, or a combination of miticidal ear drops

combined with whole-body flea-control preparations.

Demodicosis, sometimes referred to as red mange, can be one of the most difficult forms of mange to treat. Part of the problem has to do with the fact that the mites live in the hair follicles and they are relatively well shielded from topical and systemic products. The main issue, however, is that demodectic mange typically results only when there is some underlying process interfering with the dog's immune system.

Since *Demodex* mites are normal residents of the skin of

mammals, including humans, there is usually a mite population explosion only when the immune system fails to keep the number of mites in check. In young animals, the immune deficit may be transient or may reflect an actual inherited immune problem. In older animals, demodicosis is usually seen only when there is another disease hampering the immune system, such as diabetes, cancer, thyroid problems or the use of immune-suppressing drugs. Accordingly, treatment involves not only trying to kill the mange mites but also discerning what is interfering with immune function and correcting it if possible.

Chiggers represent several different species of mite that don't parasitize dogs specifically, but do latch on to passersby and can cause irritation. The problem is most prevalent in wooded areas in the late summer and fall. Treatment is not difficult, as the mites do not complete their life cycle on dogs and are susceptible to a variety of miticidal products.

MOSQUITOES

Mosquitoes have long been known to transmit a variety of diseases to people, as well as just being biting pests during warm weather. They also pose a real risk to pets. Not only do they carry deadly heartworms but

ILLUSTRATION BY PHOTOTAKE.

Illustration of **Demodex folliculoram.**

recently there also has been much concern over their involvement with West Nile virus. While we can avoid heartworm with the use of preventive medications, there are no such preventives for West Nile virus. The only method of prevention in endemic areas is active mosquito control. Fortunately, most dogs that have been exposed to the virus only developed flu-like symptoms and, to date, there have not been the large number of reported deaths in canines as seen in some other species.

MOSQUITO REPELLENT

Low concentrations of DEET (less than 10%), found in many human mosquito repellents, have been safely used in dogs but, in these concentrations, probably give only about two hours of protection. DEET may be safe in these small concentrations, but since it is not licensed for use on dogs, there is no research proving its safety for dogs. Products containing permethrin give the longest-lasting protection, perhaps two to four weeks. As DEET is not licensed for use on dogs, and both DEET and permethrin can be quite toxic to cats, appropriate care should be exercised. Other products, such as those containing oil of citronella, also have some mosquito-repellent activity, but typically have a relatively short duration of action.

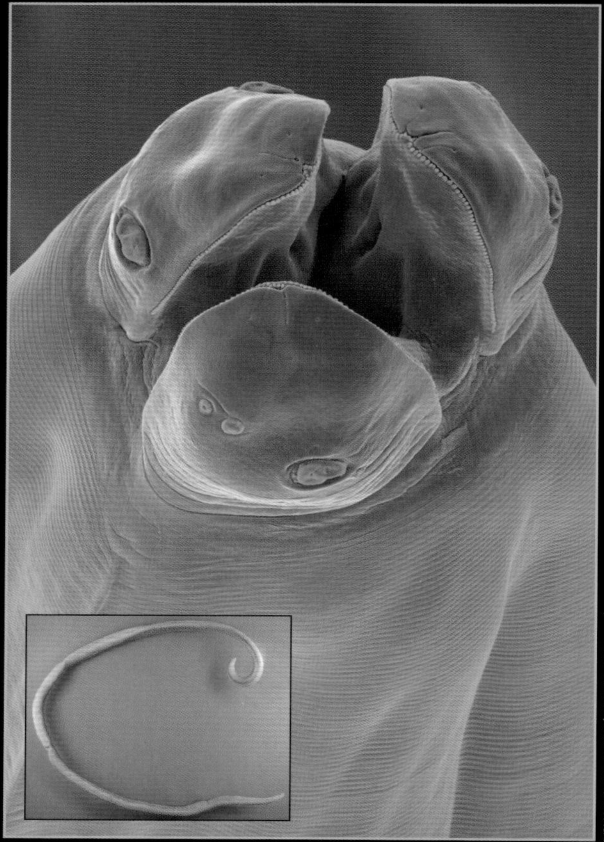

S. E. M. by Dr. Dennis Kunkel, University of Hawaii; Inset by Tam C. Nguyen.

ASCARID DANGERS

The most commonly encountered worms in dogs are roundworms known as ascarids. *Toxascaris leonine* and *Toxocara canis* are the two species that infect dogs. Subsisting in the dog's stomach and intestines, adult roundworms can grow to 7 inches in length and adult females can lay in excess of 200,000 eggs in a single day.

In humans, visceral larval migrans affects people who have ingested eggs of *Toxocara canis*, which frequently contaminates children's sandboxes, beaches and park grounds. The roundworms reside in the human's stomach and intestines, as they would in a dog's, but do not mature. Instead, they find their way to the liver, lungs and skin, or even to the heart or kidneys in severe cases. Deworming puppies is critical in preventing the infection in humans, and young children should never handle nursing pups who have not been dewormed.

The ascarid roundworm *Toxocara canis*, showing the mouth with three lips. INSET: Photomicrograph of the roundworm *Ascaris lumbricoides*.

INTERNAL PARASITES: WORMS

Ascarids

Ascarids are intestinal roundworms that rarely cause severe disease in dogs. Nonetheless, they are of major public health significance because they can be transferred to people. Sadly, it is children who are most commonly affected by the parasite, probably from inadvertently ingesting ascarid-contaminated soil. In fact, many yards and children's sandboxes contain appreciable numbers of ascarid eggs. So, while ascarids don't bite dogs or latch onto their intestines to suck blood, they do cause some nasty medical conditions in children and are best eradicated from our furry friends. Because pups can start passing ascarid eggs by three weeks of age, most parasite-control programs begin at two weeks of age and are repeated every two weeks until pups are eight weeks old. It is important to

HOOKED ON ANCYLOSTOMA

Adult dogs can become infected by the bloodsucking nematodes we commonly call hookworms via ingesting larvae from the ground or via the larvae penetrating the dog's skin. It is not uncommon for infected dogs to show no symptoms of hookworm infestation. Sometimes symptoms occur within ten days of exposure. These symptoms can include bloody diarrhea, anemia, loss of weight and general weakness. Dogs pass the hookworm eggs in their stools, which serves as the vet's method of identifying the infestation. The hookworm larvae can encyst themselves in the dog's tissues and be released when the dog is experiencing stress.

Caused by an *Ancylostoma* species whose common host is the dog, cutaneous larval migrans affects humans, causing itching and lumps and streaks beneath the surface of the skin.

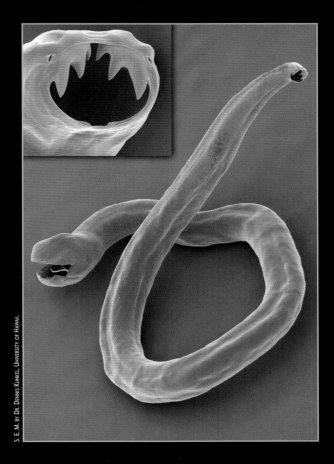

S. E. M. BY DR. DENNIS KUNKEL, UNIVERSITY OF HAWAII.

realize that bitches can pass ascarids to their pups even if they test negative prior to whelping. Accordingly, bitches are best treated at the same time as the pups.

HOOKWORMS

Unlike ascarids, hookworms do latch onto a dog's intestinal tract and can cause significant loss of blood and protein. Similar to ascarids, hookworms can be transmitted to humans, where they cause a condition known as cutaneous larval migrans. Dogs can become infected either by consuming the infective larvae or by the larvae's penetrating the skin directly. People most often get infected when they are lying on the ground (such as on a beach) and the larvae penetrate the skin. Yes, the larvae can penetrate through a beach blanket. Hookworms are typically susceptible to the same medications used to treat ascarids.

The hookworm *Ancylostoma caninum* infests the intestines of dogs. INSET: Note the row of hooks at the posterior end, used to anchor the worm to the intestinal wall.

WHIPWORMS

Whipworms latch onto the lower aspects of the dog's colon and can cause cramping and diarrhea. Eggs do not start to appear in the dog's feces until about three months after the dog was infected. This worm has a peculiar life cycle, which makes it more difficult to control than ascarids or hookworms. The good thing is that whipworms rarely are transferred to people.

Some of the medications used to treat ascarids and hookworms are also effective against whipworms, but, in general, a separate treatment protocol is needed. Since most of the medications are effective against the adults but not the eggs or larvae, treatment is typically repeated in three weeks, and then often in three

> **WORM-CONTROL GUIDELINES**
> - Practice sanitary habits with your dog and home.
> - Clean up after your dog and don't let him sniff or eat other dogs' droppings.
> - Control insects and fleas in the dog's environment. Fleas, lice, cockroaches, beetles, mice and rats can act as hosts for various worms.
> - Prevent dogs from eating uncooked meat, raw poultry and dead animals.
> - Keep dogs and children from playing in sand and soil.
> - Kennel dogs on cement or gravel; avoid dirt runs.
> - Administer heartworm preventives regularly.
> - Have your vet examine your dog's stools at your annual visits.
> - Select a boarding kennel carefully so as to avoid contamination from other dogs or an unsanitary environment.
> - Prevent dogs from roaming. Obey local leash laws.

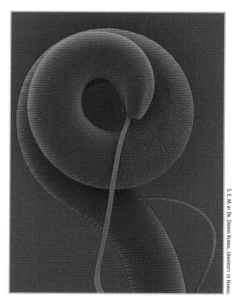

Adult whipworm, *Trichuris* sp., an intestinal parasite.

S. E. M. BY DR. DENNIS KUNKEL, UNIVERSITY OF HAWAII

months as well. Unfortunately, since dogs don't develop resistance to whipworms, it is difficult to prevent them from getting reinfected if they visit soil contaminated with whipworm eggs.

TAPEWORMS

There are many different species of tapeworm that affect dogs, but *Dipylidium caninum* is probably the most common and is spread by fleas. Flea larvae feed on organic debris and tapeworm eggs in the environment and, when a dog chews at himself and manages to ingest fleas, he might get a dose of tapeworm at the same time. The tapeworm then develops further in the intestine of the dog.

The tapeworm itself, which is a parasitic flatworm that latches onto the intestinal wall, is composed of numerous segments. When the segments break off into the intestine (as proglottids), they may accumulate around the rectum, like grains of rice. While this tapeworm is disgusting in its behavior, it is not directly communicable to humans (although humans can also get infected by swallowing fleas).

A much more dangerous flatworm is *Echinococcus multilocularis*, which is typically found in foxes, coyotes and wolves. The eggs are passed in the feces and infect rodents, and when dogs eat the rodents, the dogs can be infected by thousands of adult tapeworms. While the parasites don't cause many problems in dogs, this is considered the most lethal worm infection that people can get. Take appropriate precautions if you live in an area in which these tapeworms are found. Do not use mulch that may contain feces of dogs, cats or wildlife, and discourage your pets from hunting

wildlife. Treat these tapeworm infections aggressively in pets, because if humans get infected, approximately half die.

HEARTWORMS

Heartworm disease is caused by the parasite *Dirofilaria immitis* and is seen in dogs around the world. A member of the roundworm group, it is spread between dogs by the bite of an infected mosquito. The mosquito injects infective larvae into the dog's skin with its bite, and these larvae develop under the skin for a period of time before making their way to the heart. There they develop into adults, which grow and create blockages of the heart, lungs and major blood vessels there. They also start

A dog tapeworm proglottid (body segment).

S. E. M. BY DR. DENNIS KUNKEL, UNIVERSITY OF HAWAII.

The dog tapeworm *Taenia pisiformis*.

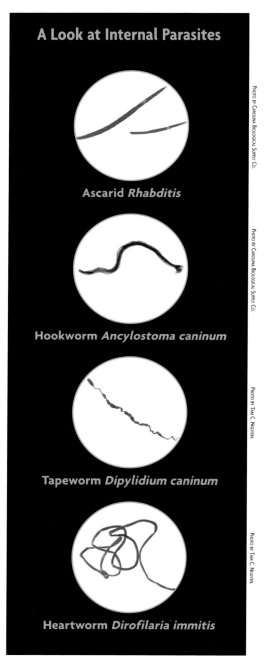

A Look at Internal Parasites

Ascarid *Rhabditis*

Hookworm *Ancylostoma caninum*

Tapeworm *Dipylidium caninum*

Heartworm *Dirofilaria immitis*

PHOTO BY CAROLINA BIOLOGICAL SUPPLY CO.

PHOTO BY CAROLINA BIOLOGICAL SUPPLY CO.

PHOTO BY TAM C. NGUYEN

PHOTO BY TAM C. NGUYEN

producing offspring (microfilariae), and these microfilariae circulate in the bloodstream, waiting to hitch a ride when the next mosquito bites. Once in the mosquito, the microfilariae develop into infective larvae and the entire process is repeated.

When dogs get infected with heartworm, over time they tend to develop symptoms associated with heart disease, such as coughing, exercise intolerance and potentially many other manifestations. Diagnosis is confirmed by either seeing the microfilariae themselves in blood samples or using immunologic tests (antigen testing) to identify the presence of adult heartworms. Since antigen tests measure the presence of adult heartworms and microfilarial tests measure offspring produced by adults, neither are positive until six to seven months after the initial infection. However, the beginning of damage can occur by fifth-stage larvae as early as three months after infection. Thus it is possible for dogs to be harboring problem-causing larvae for up to three months before either type of test would identify an infection.

The good news is that there are great protocols available for preventing heartworm in dogs. Testing is critical in the process, and it is important to understand the benefits as well as the limitations of such testing. All dogs six months of age or older that have not been on continuous heartworm-preventive

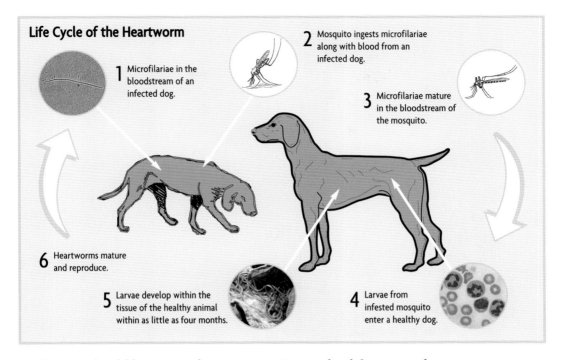

Life Cycle of the Heartworm

1 Microfilariae in the bloodstream of an infected dog.

2 Mosquito ingests microfilariae along with blood from an infected dog.

3 Microfilariae mature in the bloodstream of the mosquito.

6 Heartworms mature and reproduce.

5 Larvae develop within the tissue of the healthy animal within as little as four months.

4 Larvae from infested mosquito enter a healthy dog.

medication should be screened with microfilarial or antigen tests. For dogs receiving preventive medication, periodic antigen testing helps assess the effectiveness of the preventives. The American Heartworm Society guidelines suggest that annual retesting may not be necessary when owners have absolutely provided continuous heartworm prevention. Retesting on a two- to three-year interval may be sufficient in these cases. However, your veterinarian will likely have specific guidelines under which heartworm preventives will be prescribed, and many prefer to err on the side of safety and retest annually.

It is indeed fortunate that heartworm is relatively easy to prevent because treatments can be as life-threatening as the disease itself. Treatment requires a two-step process that kills the adult heartworms first and then the microfilariae. Prevention is obviously preferable; this involves a once-monthly oral or topical treatment. The most common oral preventives include ivermectin (not suitable for some breeds), moxidectin and milbemycin oxime; the once-a-month topical drug selamectin provides heartworm protection in addition to flea, tick and other parasite controls.

SHOWING YOUR

AFFENPINSCHER

Is dog showing in your blood? Are you excited by the idea of gaiting your handsome Affenpinscher around the ring to the thunderous applause of an enthusiastic audience? Are you certain that your beloved Affenpinscher is flawless? You are not alone! If this sounds like you, and if you are considering entering your Affenpinscher in a dog show, here are some basic questions to ask yourself:

- Did you purchase a "show-quality" puppy from the breeder?
- Is your puppy at least six months of age?
- Does the puppy exhibit correct show type for his breed?
- Does your puppy have any disqualifying faults?
- Is your Affenpinscher registered with the American Kennel Club?
- How much time do you have to devote to training, grooming,

Top-winning Ch. Yarrow's Super Nova, winning one of his many Bests in Show, this one at the Trenton Kennel Club, with handler and co-breeder Beth K. Sweigart.

conditioning and exhibiting your dog?

- Do you understand the rules and regulations of a dog show?
- Do you have time to learn how to show your dog properly?
- Do you have the financial resources to invest in showing your dog?
- Will you show the dog yourself or hire a professional handler?
- Do you have a vehicle that can accommodate your weekend trips to the dog shows?

Success in the show ring requires more than a pretty face, a waggy tail and a pocketful of liver. Even though dog shows can be exciting and enjoyable, the sport of conformation makes great demands on the exhibitors and the dogs. Winning exhibitors live for their dogs, devoting time and money to their dogs' presentation, conditioning and training. Very few novices, even those with good dogs, will find themselves in the winners' circle, though it does happen. Don't be disheartened, though. Every exhibitor began as a novice and worked his way up to the Group ring. It's the "working your way up" part that you must keep in mind.

Assuming that you have purchased a puppy of the correct type and quality for showing, let's begin to examine the world of showing and what's required to get started. Although the entry fee into a dog show is nominal, there are lots of other hidden costs involved with "finishing" your Affenpinscher, that is, making him a champion. Things like equipment, travel, training and conditioning all cost money. A more serious campaign will include fees for a professional handler, boarding, cross-country travel and advertising. Top-winning show dogs can represent a very considerable investment—over $100,000 has been spent in campaigning some dogs. (The investment can be less, of course, for owners who don't

Using a treat to capture her Affenpinscher's attention, the handler coaxes her dog to "free stand" while the judge looks him over.

use professional handlers.)

Many owners, on the other hand, enter their "average" Affenpinschers in dog shows for the fun and enjoyment of it. Dog showing makes an absorbing hobby, with many rewards for dogs and owners alike. If you're having fun, meeting other people who share your interests and enjoying the overall experience, you likely will catch the "bug." Soon you will be envisioning yourself in the center ring at the Westminster Kennel Club Dog Show in New York City, competing for the prestigious Best in Show cup.

AKC CONFORMATION SHOWING

GETTING STARTED

Visiting a dog show as a spectator is a great place to start. Pick up the show catalog to find out what time your breed is being shown, who is judging the breed and in which ring the classes will be held. To start, Affenpinschers compete against other Affenpinschers, and the winner is selected as Best of Breed by the judge. This is the procedure for each breed. At a group show, all of the Best of Breed winners go on to compete for Group One in their respective groups. For example, all Best of Breed winners in a given group compete against each other; this is done for all seven groups. Finally, all seven group winners go head to head in the ring for the Best in Show award.

What most spectators don't understand is the basic idea of conformation. A dog show is often referred as a "conformation" show. This means that the judge should decide how each dog stacks up (conforms) to the breed standard for his given breed: how well does this Affenpinscher conform to the ideal representative detailed in the standard? Ideally, this is what happens. In reality, however, this ideal often gets slighted as the judge compares Affenpinscher #1

Standing tall and proud in his silver cup is Ch. Yarrow's Mighty Joe Young, winning Best in Show at the Penn Ridge Kennel Club. Owners, Dr. and Mrs. William Truesdale. Handler, Beth K. Sweigart.

to Affenpinscher #2. Again, the ideal is that each dog is judged based on his merits in comparison to his breed standard, not in comparison to the other dogs in the ring. It is easier for judges to compare dogs of the same breed to decide which they think is the better specimen; in the Group and Best in Show ring, however, it is very difficult to compare one breed to another, like apples to oranges. Thus the dog's conformation to the breed standard—not to mention advertising dollars and good handling—is essential to success in conforma-

The judge carefully reviews the line of Affenpinschers as they stand in show pose, looking their best.

tion shows. The dog described in the standard is the perfect dog of that breed, and breeders keep their eye on the standard when they choose which dogs to breed, hoping to get closer and closer to the ideal with each litter.

Another good first step for the novice is to join a dog club. You will be astonished by the many and different kinds of dog clubs in the country, with about 5,000 clubs holding events every year. Perhaps you've made some friends visiting a show held by a particular club and you would like to join that club. Dog clubs may specialize in a single breed, like a local or regional Affenpinscher club, or in a specific pursuit, such as obedience, tracking or agility. There are all-breed clubs for all dog enthusiasts; they sponsor special training days,

MEET THE AKC

The American Kennel Club is the main governing body of the dog sport in the United States. Founded in 1884, the AKC consists of 500 or more independent dog clubs plus 4,500 affiliated clubs, all of which follow the AKC rules and regulations. Additionally, the AKC maintains a registry for pure-bred dogs in the US and works to preserve the integrity of the sport and its continuation in the country. Over 1,000,000 dogs are registered each year, representing over 150 recognized breeds. There are over 15,000 competitive events held annually for which over 2,000,000 dogs enter to participate. Dogs compete to earn over 40 different titles, from Champion to Companion Dog to Master Agility Champion.

Small dogs like Affenpinschers are examined by the judge on a table, to raise the dogs to a suitable height and allow for the required hands-on evaluation.

seminars on topics like grooming or handling or lectures on breeding or canine genetics. There are also clubs that specialize in certain types of dogs, like toy dogs, hunting dogs, herding dogs, etc.

A parent club is the national organization, sanctioned by the AKC, which promotes and safeguards its breed in the country. The Affenpinscher Club of America was formed in 1965 and can be contacted on the Internet at www.affenpinscher.org. The parent club holds an annual national specialty show, usually in a different city each year, in which many of the country's top dogs, handlers and breeders gather to compete. At a specialty

show, only members of a single breed are invited to participate. There are also group specialties, in which all members of a group are invited. For more information about dog clubs in your area, contact the AKC at www.akc.org on the Internet or write them at their Raleigh, NC address.

HOW SHOWS ARE ORGANIZED
Three kinds of conformation shows are offered by the AKC. There is the all-breed show, in which all AKC-recognized breeds can compete; the specialty show, which is for one breed only and usually sponsored by the breed's parent club and the group show, for all breeds in one of the AKC's seven groups. The Affenpinscher competes in the Toy Group.

FOR MORE INFORMATION...
For reliable up-to-date information about registration, dog shows and other canine competitions, contact one of the national registries by mail or via the Internet.

American Kennel Club
5580 Centerview Dr., Raleigh, NC 27606-3390
www.akc.org

United Kennel Club
100 E. Kilgore Road, Kalamazoo, MI 49002
www.ukcdogs.com

Canadian Kennel Club
89 Skyway Ave., Suite 100, Etobicoke, Ontario
M9W 6R4 Canada
www.ckc.ca

For a dog to become an AKC champion of record, the dog must earn 15 points at shows. The points must be awarded by at least three different judges and must include two "majors" under different judges. A "major" is a three-, four- or five-point win, and the number of points per win is determined by the number of dogs competing in the show on that day. (Dogs that are absent or are excused are not counted.) The number of points that are awarded varies from breed to breed. More dogs are needed to attain a major in more popular breeds, and fewer dogs are needed in less popular breeds. Yearly, the AKC evaluates the number of dogs in competition in each division (there are 14 divisions in all, based on geography) and may or may not change the numbers of dogs required for each number of points. For example, a major in Division 2 (Delaware, New Jersey and Pennsylvania) recently required 17 dogs or 16 bitches for a three-point major, 29 dogs or 27 bitches for a four-point major and 51 dogs or 46 bitches for a five-point major. The Affenpinscher attracts numerically proportionate representation at all-breed shows.

Only one dog and one bitch of each breed can win points at a given show. There are no "co-ed" classes except for champions of

One of the top-winning Affenpinschers in the US, Ch. Hilane's Lonesome Cowboy with the author, Jerome Cushman, his proud owner/handler.

record. Dogs and bitches do not compete against each other until they are champions. Dogs that are not champions (referred to as "class dogs") compete in one of five classes. The class in which a dog is entered depends on age and previous show wins. First there is the Puppy Class (sometimes divided further into classes for 6- to 9-month-olds and 9- to 12-month-olds); next is the

The Affenpinscher's gait according to the standard should be "light, free, sound, balanced, confident," carrying himself with "comic seriousness."

Novice Class (for dogs that have no points toward their championships and whose only first-place wins have come in the Puppy Class or the Novice Class, the latter class limited to three first places); then there is the American-bred Class (for dogs bred in the US); the Bred-by-Exhibitor Class (for dogs handled by their breeders or by immediate family members of their breeders) and the Open Class (for any non-champions). Any dog may enter the Open Class, regardless of age or win history, but to be competitive the dog should be older and have ring experience.

The judge at the show begins judging the male dogs in the Puppy Class(es) and proceeds through the other classes. The judge awards first through fourth place in each class. The first-place winners of each class then compete with one another in the Winners Class to determine Winners Dog. The judge then starts over with the bitches, beginning with the Puppy Class(es) and proceeding up to the Winners Class to award Winners Bitch, just as he did with the dogs. A Reserve Winners Dog and Reserve Winners Bitch are also selected; they could be awarded the points in the case of a disqualification.

The Winners Dog and Winners Bitch are the two that are awarded the points for their breed. They then go on to compete with any champions of record (often called "specials") of their breed that are entered in the show. The champions may be dogs or bitches; in this class, all are shown together. The judge reviews the Winners Dog and Winners Bitch along with all of the champions to select the Best of Breed winner. The Best of Winners is selected between the Winners Dog and Winners Bitch; if one of these two is selected Best of Breed as well, he or she is automatically determined Best of Winners. Lastly, the judge selects Best of Opposite Sex to the Best of Breed winner. The Best of Breed winner then goes on to the group competition.

At a group or all-breed show, the Best of Breed winners from each breed are divided into their respective groups to compete against one another for Group One through Group Four. Group One (first place) is awarded to the dog that best lives up to the ideal for his breed as described in the standard. A group judge, therefore, must have a thorough working knowledge of many breed standards. After placements have been made in each group, the seven Group One winners (from the Toy Group, Sporting Group, Hound Group, etc.) compete against each other for the top honor, Best in Show.

There are different ways to find out about dog shows in your area. The American Kennel Club's monthly magazine, the *American Kennel Gazette* is accompanied by the *Events Calendar*; this magazine is available through subscription. You can also look on the AKC's and your parent club's websites for information and check the event listings in your local newspaper.

Your Affenpinscher must be six months of age or older and registered with the AKC in order to be entered in AKC-sanctioned

The top Affenpinscher in Canada, here's Ch. Hilane's Harry Potter, receiving an Award of Merit at the 2005 national specialty in the US. Owner, Sandra Lex.

**CANINE GOOD CITIZEN®
PROGRAM**
Have you ever considered getting
your dog "certified"? The AKC's
Canine Good Citizen® Program
affords your dog just that
opportunity. Your dog shows that he
is a well-behaved canine citizen,
using the basic training and good
manners you have taught him, by
taking a series of ten tests that
illustrate that he can behave properly
at home, in a public place and around
other dogs. The tests are
administered by participating dog
clubs, colleges, 4-H clubs, Scouts and
other community groups and are
open to all pure-bred and mixed-
breed dogs. Upon passing the ten
tests, the suffix CGC is then applied
to your dog's name.

The ten tests are: 1. Accepting a
friendly stranger; 2. Sitting politely
for petting; 3. Appearance and
grooming; 4. Walking on a lead; 5.
Walking through a group of people;
6. Sit, down and stay on command; 7.
Coming when called; 8. Meeting
another dog; 9. Calm reaction to
distractions; 10. Separation from
owner.

which dogs and bitches are
worthy of being bred. Therefore if
they cannot be bred, that defeats
the purpose! On that note, only
dogs that have achieved championships, thus proving their excellent quality, should be bred. If you
have spayed or neutered your dog,
however, there are many AKC
events other than conformation,
such as obedience trials, agility
trials and the Canine Good
Citizen® Program, in which you
and your Affenpinscher can
participate.

You're at the Show, Now What?
You will fill out an entry form
when you register for the show.
You must decide and designate on
the form in which class you will
enter your puppy or adult dog.
Remember that some classes are
more competitive than others and
have limitations based on age and
win history. Hopefully you will
not be in the first class of the day,
so you can take some time watching exactly how the judge is
conducting the ring. Notice how
the handlers are stacking their
dogs, meaning setting them up in
a standing pose. Does the judge
prefer the dogs to be facing one
direction or another? Take special
note as to how the judge is
moving the dogs and how he is
instructing the handlers. Is he
moving them up and back, once
or twice around, in a triangle?

If possible, you will want to

shows in which there are classes
for the Affenpinscher. Your Affenpinscher also must not possess
any disqualifying faults and must
be sexually intact. The reason for
the latter is simple: dog shows are
the proving grounds to determine

get your number beforehand. Your assigned number must be attached as an armband or with a clip on your outer garment. Do not enter the ring without your number. The ring steward will usually call the exhibits in numerical order. If the exhibits are not called in order, you should strategically place your dog in the line. For instance, if your pup is small for his age, don't stand him next to a large entry; if your dog is reluctant to gait, get at the end of the line-up so that you don't interfere with the other dogs. The judge's first direction, usually, is for all of the handlers to "take the dogs around," which means that everyone gaits his dog around the periphery of the ring.

While you're in the ring, don't let yourself (or your dog) become distracted. Concentrate on your dog; he should have your full attention. Stack him in the best way possible. Teach him to free-stand while you hold a treat out for him. Let him understand that he must hold this position for at least a minute before you reward him. Follow the judge's instructions and be aware of what the judge is doing. Don't frustrate the judge by not paying attention to his directions.

When your dog's turn to be judged arrives, keep him steady and calm. The judge will inspect the dog's bite and dentition, overall musculature and structure and, in a male dog, the testicles, which must completely descend into the scrotum. Likewise, the judge will take note of the dog's alertness and temperament. Aggressiveness is a disqualification in most breeds and so is shyness. A dog must always be approachable by the judge, even if aloofness is one of the breed's characteristics. Once the judge has completed his hands-on inspection, he will instruct you to gait the dog. A dog's gait indicates to the judge

Winning the group at the Tonawanda Valley Kennel Club is Ch. Yarrow's Over the Moon, handled by Jerome Cushman. The judge is Michele Billings.

GROUP 1ST

TONAWANDA VALLEY KENNEL CLUB
Sept. 2, 2001
© J.C. Photography

McNULTY DOG SHOWS

that the dog is correctly constructed. Each breed standard describes the ideal correct gait for that breed. After the judge has inspected all of the dogs in the class in this manner, he will ask the entire class to gait together. He will make his final selections after one last look over the class.

Whether you win or lose, the only one disappointed will be you. Never let your dog know that he's not "the winner." Most important is that you reaffirm your dog's love of the game.

Top-ten Toy Dog Ch. Tamarin Tip-Off, the number-one Affenpinscher for 2005, goes by "Buzz."

PHOTO BY NANCY SPIELE, CUSTOM DOG DESIGNS.

Reward him for behaving properly and for being the handsome boy or pretty girl that he or she is.

After your first or second experience in the ring, you will know what things you need to work on. Go home, practice and have fun with your Affenpinscher. With some time and effort, you and your well-trained show dog will soon be standing in the winners' circle with a blue ribbon!

As a six-month-old youngster, here's where "Cosmos" began. He ended up the top-winning Affenpinscher in history, known as Ch. Yarrow's Super Nova.

INDEX

My Affenpinscher

PUT YOUR PUPPY'S FIRST PICTURE HERE

Dog's Name _____

Date _____ Photographer _____